S0-BID-715

B.C.

BR 1725 .N5 L3
Langenskjöld, Margareta, 1889-
Baron Paul Nicolay

BARON PAUL NICOLAY

A Biography

BARON PAUL NICOLAY

BARON PAUL NICOLAY

*Christian Statesman and Student Leader in
Northern and Slavic Europe*

BY

GRETA LANGENSKJOLD

Translated from the Swedish by
RUTH EVELYN WILDER

ILLUSTRATED

3735
NEW YORK
GEORGE H. DORAN COMPANY

CALIFORNIA BAPTIST THEOLOGICAL SEMINARY
AUDITORIUM BUILDING
LOS ANGELES 13, CALIFORNIA

BR
1725
.N5
L3

COPYRIGHT, 1924,
BY GEORGE H. DORAN COMPANY

79479

BARON PAUL NICOLAY
— B —
PRINTED IN THE UNITED STATES OF AMERICA

FOREWORD

By MISS RUTH ROUSE

SECRETARY TO THE EXECUTIVE COMMITTEE OF THE WORLD'S
STUDENT CHRISTIAN FEDERATION

PIONEER work in connection with the World's
Student Christian Federation brought me into a close
fellowship of work with Baron Nicolay during a
period of twelve years, 1903-1915. The years that
have passed since we last met have thrown details
into the background. Only the more clearly do I see
in the foreground the strong main features of Paul
Nicolay's work and character. As I meditate on these,
two words spring to mind:

*"It is required in stewards that they be found faith-
ful."* Above all things and in all things Paul Nicolay
"kept the faith": faith to God, faith to man, faith to
his call. Once having seen a thing to be true, he lived
by that sight unwaveringly; once having heard a call,
he answered at all hazards; once having made a promise, he kept it at all costs. As a study in the meaning
of Vocation and Stewardship, Paul Nicolay's life
will help hundreds to find their own life-work, and to
carry it through, come what may.

"His works do follow him." Paul Nicolay's work
did not end in 1919. He gave his life to and for the
Russian Student Christian Movement, and in its life
he lives to-day. Since his death that movement has

passed through famine, dungeon, fire and sword. It is still under the harrow. But it is stronger than ever; like its founder, it cannot be discouraged, it cannot take its hand from the plough. It has heard a clear call and has no thought but to obey.

He lives again in its leaders. Almost all the younger Russian leaders of the Movement, and of similar movements amongst the Russian Diaspora, are men and women whose spiritual life owes very much to their contact with Baron Nicolay and to his faithful shepherding of their souls. In Bulgaria, in Prague, in the Baltic States, they are passing on what he taught them by word and life. "Doesn't he remind you of Baron Nicolay?" we say to each other, as we see the way they work.

But not Russians alone learnt to know God through him. Swedes, Finlanders, Norwegians, English, Americans—from all these I have heard the same testimony: "I shall never forget what Baron Nicolay said at ——— Conference." "I shall never lose the impression Baron Nicolay made on me." The strongest evangelist in the Bulgarian Orthodox Church today is one of his disciples, a Bulgarian, who did his theological studies in Russia, was a member of the Movement there and gratefully acknowledges his debt to its leader.

The best one can wish for this book is that it should pass on to thousands more that Call to Faithfulness which Paul Nicolay gave to so many in his lifetime.

Wimbledon,
    London, S. W.

CONTENTS

ILLUSTRATIONS

BARON PAUL NICOLAY

A Biography

BARON PAUL NICOLAY

CHAPTER I

Ancestry

"SUSTINE et abstine"—these words formed the motto emblazoned on the coat of arms of the Nicolay family, and a silver cross on a blue field and surrounded by four golden stars was their sign. No better motto nor more inspiring device could the last of the Nicolays—he whose life we are about to depict—have chosen for himself, if the choice had been his to make. From his ancestors he inherited them as well as many of the characteristics which formed the nucleus of his being throughout his life: earnestness, faithfulness, and a tendency toward simple rigorous habits. These characteristics became a useful antidote to the other half of his inheritance which was calculated to afford his character many a hard test: the inherited position of the cosmopolitan, the man of the world, the possessor of entail property of great value.

The Nicolays originated in Sweden, but as early as the year 1500 one of the family moved to Lübeck, and one hundred and twenty-five years later we find his descendants in Alsace, in Strassburg. Here, in the year 1737, Ludwig Heinrich Nicolay was born, he

who was to become the father of this line of nobility.
He was the son of a stern and despotically minded
magistrate, and according to the will of his father entered upon a legal course of studies. Throughout his
whole life, however, he maintained his great literary
and artistic interests. After finishing his university
course he was sent to Paris, bringing with him letters
of introduction to the French encyclopedists—d'Alem-
bert and Diderot—which helped to bring him into
touch with a brilliant and gifted circle of acquaintances. The young man enjoyed it without letting it
injure his character, for the strong religious principles which were the basis of his upbringing now
showed forth in their full strength. Says his German
biographer: "Equipped with this shield he was able
to resist Diderot himself; yes, he even succeeded at
a dinner in a tête-à-tête with this man, the most cor-
rupt of all the encyclopedists, through his simple and
direct answers to religious questions, especially those
concerning his own beliefs, in persuading him to abandon the thought of winning him over to the new ideas
without its affecting their friendly intercourse together."

Several years later Ludwig Heinrich moved to
Vienna, where he became the private secretary of the
Russian Ambassador, Count Rasumovsky, whom he
later accompanied to Italy. In 1769 he was admitted
by Count Parien into the service of the Russian court.
In this way the Alsatian moved into the great Empire
of the East, where he settled and where, thanks to
his great ability and his strong character, he succeeded
in creating for himself and his family an honourable

and, considering the conditions of the time, an unusually secure position. At the court he was at first
tutor of Grand Duke Paul, then heir to the throne,
and during the latter's reign he became his private
secretary. After the death of the Emperor Paul he
remained the secretary to his widow, Empress Maria
Feodorovna. In 1782 the honour of the name of
Von Nicolay was conferred on Ludwig Heinrich by
the Emperor Josef II of Austria. The title of Baron
was conferred on him in Russia. He was also appointed Privy Councillor and for some time held the
position of President of the Academy of Science.

As early as the year 1788 Ludwig Heinrich Nicolay
had bought from the Duke of Württemberg, governor
of the province of Wiborg, the castle Monrepos, sit-
uated in the parish of Wiborg in Finland, and formerly known as Lill-Ladugård. He had acquired by
purchase the possession of this crown property. Nevertheless, it was not until 1801 that Baron Nicolay
secured the full right to possession of the estate
through imperial rescript. Ludwig Heinrich, as well
as many of his descendants, became greatly attached
to the home at Monrepos, and in this way a bond—
although at first merely of an outward nature—was
gradually formed binding them to Finland. In beautifying Monrepos' already beautiful parks through
ingenious decorations bearing the impress of love and
good taste, Ludwig Heinrich found an outlet for his
intrinsic artistic inclinations. The first Baron Nicolay was known as the author of several poems and
fables in the spirit of the time, and he even sang to
the praise of his beloved park in a poem entitled "Das

Landgut Monrepos." On the beautiful little island
of Ludwigstein which belongs to the estate, and
which with its high rocky walls and cypress-like firs
reminds the modern visitor very strongly of the
artist Böcklin's picture "The Isle of Death," can also
be found engraved in a marble column two lines written by the poetic ancestor:

> *"Auf kurze Zeit ist dieser Hügel mein,*
> *Auf lange Zeit bin ich dann sein."*

Ludwigstein was set aside as a real "isle of death"
for the members of the Nicolay family, and a more
beautiful or more peaceful burial ground could hardly
be found in any spot throughout the world. The
scenery of Monrepos, beautified by a loving hand,
and the poetic writings of the first Baron Nicolay
bear witness to his cultural interests. The extensive
collection of books, which for long formed one of
the treasures of the estate and which can now be
found in the University Library of Helsingfors, was
made by him in conjunction with a friend of his
youth, the Frenchman Lafermière, who was at one
time tutor of the Emperor Paul, as well as librarian
and theatre director. The collection of books, called
"Bibliothèque des deux amis," fell, according to
mutual agreement, after his friend's death to the lot
of Baron Nicolay.

Ludwig Heinrich was lovable, friendly and depend-
able. The last years of his life were spent in retire-
ment in the country at Monrepos with his wife,
Johanna Poggenpohl, the daughter of a German

banker. They had a very happy married life together and both died in the same year, 1820. Their only son, Paul, born in 1777, had at the age of eight been sent by his father to the famous author Joh. Heinr. Voss, rector at Eutin near Lübeck. Here he grew up with the learned man's sons and imbibed in this atmosphere a love for the classics which was his throughout life. Later he studied at the University at Erlangen and did not return home until he was eighteen years of age. He then entered upon a diplomatic career and traveled to London, where he served for several years under Count Vorontsov. After coming back to Russia he took part, among other things, in a commission whose purpose was to fix Finland's boundary in the direction of Sweden and Norway. In 1811 he married Alexandrine Simplicie de Broglie, daughter of a French refugee, Prince de Broglie, who belonged to one branch of the famous ducal family of this name.

The family de Broglie were known to be very pious Roman Catholics, and Princess Alexandrine brought with her as a gift to the family of which she now became a member something of this deep religious spirit. After her father's death in Germany where the fugitives first went, her mother and her three brothers sought with her a home in Russia. Alexandrine received her education at the school in Smolna. Her brothers became pages at the court and later fought as officers of the guard against Napoleon. The eldest of them fell at Austerlitz and the youngest perished at Kulm in 1813, so that only one of the Princes de Broglie was able to return to the home country with his mother after the restoration. Among the many monuments of special interest in the park at Monrepos which speak of a peaceful, dreamy restfulness, is found the so-called Broglie monument, a stately obelisk of Swedish marble erected on an eminence to the memory of the two young Frenchmen who had lost their lives. In the solitude of this quiet spot it speaks of the boisterous life of the great world where so much is going on, yet without disturbing the surrounding harmony which it rather seems to enhance. Thus, even though the family at Monrepos has received influences and impressions from many different directions, it has always succeeded in assimilating them, so that the family chronicles without being colourless yet lack, to an unusual degree, the rebellious, dramatic element which is so often found in the history of a race of nobles. According to the wish of his father, Ludwig Heinrich, it was decided that the sons of Paul and Alexandrine Nicolay should belong to the Lutheran Church. The daughters, on the contrary, were to be brought up in their mother's religion, so that no cause for disagreement between the parents might arise. Paul Nicolay was very fond of his wife, and his sorrow was great when in the year 1829 death tore her away from him and their seven little children. Prior to her death she had not had the strength to speak to her husband about the future, but she wrote many farewell letters exhorting him bravely to bear his grief and to bring up his children in the Christian faith. "Sois plus qu'un homme, sois un chrétien résigné." Thus ended her last letter to him, and these words were later placed by the widower over his deceased wife's portrait. The commission, which Paul Nicolay thus received from his "conjux amantissima, dulcissima, piissima, amica fidelissima," as she is called in the Latin memorial on her grave, he carried out faithfully, and became a good father who implanted in his children the same dependability of character which was so marked in him. In order to give his daughters the advantages of a mother's care and to fulfil his promise to his wife that they should grow up in a Roman Catholic atmosphere, he entrusted them for several years to the care of their grandmother in Normandy.

In 1822 Paul Nicolay became a Finnish Baron, and the family in the year 1828 was the thirtieth to enter the House of Nobles. Several years later he received the notification of the testamental statute whereby Monrepos estate became entail in nature to be handed down to his descendants. At the age of seventy he retired to his beloved estate where he lived until the year of his death, 1866, tenderly cared for by his unmarried daughter Simplicie. After her father's death Simplicie entered a convent in Normandy, which, however, never hindered her from thinking of her own people with deep affection. Her many letters as well as the joy she always showed when any of her relatives visited her bear witness to this. Simplicie was, however, not the only one of the family to leave the world for a convent life. Her brother Louis, the second in age, became in later life a Roman Catholic, thereby exposing himself to the disfavour of the Russian Government. In 1868 he interrupted a brilliant military career—for at the age of forty-eight he had

been advanced to the position of Adjutant-general besides having taken part with distinction in many campaigns—in order to enter the famous Carthusian
Monastery near Grenoble, "La Grande Chartreuse."
Here he studied theology, and was later ordained.
But he also kept on intimate terms with his family,
the younger members of which, among whom was his
nephew Paul, often visited him during their foreign
travels.

The youngest of the brothers, Alexander, who
studied at the "Imperial Lyceum" at Tsarskoje Selo
and prepared for the position of a government official,
remained in Russia and held through a succession of
years several high positions. He became Chamberlain, head of the civil administration of Tiflis in the
Caucasus, and was later a member of the Council of
Empire, and finally Minister of Education. He only
held this latter position for a year because he dared
to oppose the Russianisation policy of the then omnip-
otent Procurator of the Holy Synod, Pobjedo-
nostsev, and of the other ministers with reference
to foreigners in the Empire. He remained after that
a member of the Council of Empire until the year
1889, when he resigned and retired to Tiflis, where
resided his only daughter, who had married a Caucasian prince. He himself had married a princess,
Tsjavtsjavadse by name, but had become a widower
at an early age. He died in 1899 at his estate near
Tiflis, leaving behind him the memory of a very reserved and exceptionally industrious and conscientious
man. His punctuality, a trait of character which
reappeared in his nephew, was said to be so great

that the inhabitants of Tiflis regulated their clocks when Baron Nicolay went across the market place on his way to his Civil Service Department.

Nicholas, the eldest son of Paul and Alexandrine de Broglie, was born in 1818 in Copenhagen. He was educated at home by an excellent tutor until, at the age of 16, he became a student at the University of St. Petersburg. After completing his preparatory studies, he chose his father's career and entered the service of the Russian Embassy in Berlin, where he continued to attend lectures at the University. Later, after visiting The Hague and London, he was offered a position at the Ministry of Foreign Affairs in St. Petersburg, where he spent a couple of years. At this time he became acquainted with Sophie Meyendorff, the 18-year-old daughter of the Livonian Baron George Meyendorff and his wife, née Countess Stachelberg. He fell in love, as he himself expresses it, with the young girl's charming simplicity—"simplicité charmante," by which he was delightfully impressed. During her childhood Sophie Meyendorff had received lasting religious impressions from an English governess who was an earnest believer, and these impressions had grown still deeper while preparing for confirmation, in the quiet of the Livonian village. Nicholas Nicolay had also been brought up with a deep religious faith, so the marriage, entered into in 1853, became, despite the difference in age, a very happy one, founded as it was on common principles and life purposes. Baron Nicolay's position soon brought him and his young wife abroad, first to Berlin, where their eldest little daughter died and another was born, and then to London, Bern, and Copenhagen. At each of those places one of their children saw the light of day for the first time.

In 1866 a great change took place in the formerly so happy life of the family, for in that year the father was attacked by a severe disease which necessitated his giving up his position in order to seek a cure in the warmer climate of Germany. Hope of his recovery was, however, not realised, and after three years of great suffering he entered into the eternal rest.

The young widow, still only thirty-four years of age, moved in the spring of 1870 with her children, Marie, Aline, Sophie, and Paul, to Monrepos, the ancestral estate of her husband. Here many years were spent in quiet seclusion. But later, solicitous for her children's education, the mother moved to St. Petersburg where they could more easily receive the needed instruction and the friendly intercourse she desired. In this way the Russian capital became the place where the last male descendant of the family of Nicolay grew into manhood and found his life course and his appointed task.　　　R.

CHAPTER II

Childhood and Youth

PAUL NICOLAY was born in Bern July 14, 1860.
He spent the first years of his life in Denmark
and Germany, but later, as we have seen, his home
was moved to St. Petersburg—the brilliant metropolis
of the time, doubly brilliant to one who like him
belonged to the circle of the wealthy and the highest
social standing. It is hard to imagine an atmosphere
less suited for deepening spiritual growth and for the
normal development of a religious nature. St. Petersburg before the Revolution always had countless intellectual and artistic pleasures to offer the prosperous
portion of her inhabitants as lighter diversions, and
the life of St. Petersburg with its mixture of the
national and the cosmopolitan, of Russian unaffected-
ness and foreign refinement, has held for many a
special charm, an almost irresistible power of attraction. But the nervous strain, which always characterised this life, seldom permitted that quiet concentration of mind which is alone favourable to the growth
of the soul. Paul Nicolay was indeed fortunate to
find in his home from the very beginning a wholesome
antidote to the superficiality of the large city. Here,
day by day, the boy was influenced by a spirit entirely
opposed to the more or less brilliant immorality which
he otherwise met in so many places. The centre and
leading force of the home was the mother.

Baroness Sophie Nicolay was in many respects a most exceptional personality. The hard trial inflicted on her by her husband's serious illness and early death served to deepen within her the spiritual life already so rich in her youth. A genuine cordiality and sincere conscientiousness about even the smallest things distinguished her character, giving a loving harmony to her whole life. Her great humility was combined in a unique way with an imposing dignity of bearing. The shyness, which never entirely left her—a characteristic inherited by her son—occasionally gave the appearance of coldness, but this impression soon disappeared before the sincere, simple spirit of kindliness with which she treated high and low alike, and which gradually won the hearts of all. She was the centre of her children's affection. With a firm and loving hand, she knew how to develop in them an alert conscience and a vital faith in God. During her stay abroad, especially during the trying experience in Germany, she had come into close fellowship with believers, and her religion had thus acquired a warmer and deeper hue than that which is typical of the usual Lutheranism. Even English influences could, as we know, be traced in her spiritual life, combining German depth of feeling with the active, characteristically practical nature of Anglo-Saxon religion.

Her devotion to God penetrated all the daily duties of life in the Nicolay home. Not only was the family gathered together daily in morning worship, but the mother sought to accustom her children at an early age to set aside at least fifteen minutes each day for individual Bible study and prayer.

The following words written by Paul Nicolay at the age of ten in a letter to his mother show how successful she had been in making this a very precious custom to her little son: "Auntie takes prayers for us in the morning, but I think it is easier to do it by myself. I will try to be good, but you must pray God to help me."

Without wishing to draw hasty conclusions from an isolated letter, it can be said that these words are very significant in showing how early Paul Nicolay came into a personal relationship with God. Typical of him in another respect is something he writes of in a letter a year later. He is telling how to his great joy he has just discovered his favourite pet of the summer, his precious turtle, which had disappeared and had now been found by the sons of the manager of the estate near the bath house at Monrepos. He writes: "How wonderful! I had just been praying to God this morning, 'If it is Thy will please let me find my turtle.'" To the contemplative child so inclined to introspection this little incident became a personal experience of faith, and the religious discipline of his prayer life is already plainly marked in the phrase "if it is Thy will." The religious nature of his mother's training helped greatly in strengthening in him that sense of loyalty to duty and that inclination to self-criticism which were inherent in the boy. One of his tutors, his arithmetic teacher, once said of his pupil, who was then thirteen, that he could not rid himself of an idea until he had fully understood it. Paul Nicolay, writing about this later, says: "This seems to me to be the right and the only good side of my character." The whole character of the boy develops wonderfully in the helpful atmosphere of the home. But his childhood days are not entirely free from clouds. Physically he is far from strong, he has a nervous temperament, and the moral battle, which he never took lightly, must even now have caused him a great deal of anxiety. The chief faults of his childhood were a hot temper and a rather capricious irritability, tendencies which he says he had to fight throughout his whole life. Even now he has declared war on them. His mother and his eldest sister, Marie, stood by him faithfully in this battle, and he therefore feels toward them a very deep and unaffected love. "Tell Marie that I read my Bible every evening," he writes in March of the year 1876 in a letter to his mother, who with her daughters was then visiting Rome. "It is marvellous how God has helped me in school so far. You can not imagine how much I miss you all! Home seems empty, for there is no one there whom I love and who loves me as you do. Good-bye, my darling Mother, there is no danger of my forgetting you. I think of you and long for you very often."

The school, which the young boy mentions here, was the "Gymnasium" of the "Historical-Philological Faculty" of St. Petersburg, an institution for training teachers, something like an American normal school. In September 1873 Paul entered this school, from which he was graduated seven years later. Prior to this he had received private instruction in various subjects. There is not much to be said about his school life. His

first impressions of school were such as might be
expected of a boy who had lived rather an isolated
life in the shelter of his home and who was suddenly
transplanted into a circle of lively and boisterous boy
companions. The first favourable judgment of the
school concerns this spirit of fun, and not the instruction. "School is great fun. We played a great many
boyish tricks, laughed, pushed each other, and made
the desks walk," he writes in a letter. These pranks,
which were certainly not foreign to young Nicolay's
nature, were soon however subordinated to the strong
sense of duty which characterised him, and he later
studied hard and distinguished himself by his excellent work at school. But this did not, however, give
him any particular joy in his work—he was too
nervous for that to be possible and maybe also too
sensitively conscientious, and the system of examinations then prevalent in Russia must have been a terrible ordeal for him. Significant are the words of
the letter quoted above: "It is marvellous how God
has helped me in school so far." Now, as later, Paul
Nicolay takes every task seriously, is always striving
for the best possible results which he often attains,
but usually at the expense of his health, and the work
rests upon his young shoulders as a great burden.
But for the most part neither the teaching nor the
companionships made any deep impression on his
personal development. This may have been due to
his keen and strongly individualistic makeup, or perhaps the atmosphere of his cosmopolitan and aristocratic home afforded, in spite of all its simplicity, too

few points of contact with the motley group of a
Russian school. At any rate, he must have felt himself
a stranger among his teachers and companions.

Of far greater significance to the youth than his
school life could ever be was the training for confirmation, which he and his youngest sister received
from the pastor of the German church in the winter
of 1879. This was hardly due to the nature of the
teaching itself, but rather to the claims which, in view
of the approaching religious decision, became personal and vital to the young candidate for confirmation. Paul Nicolay strives throughout this period
with the wholehearted intensity of an honest nature
to concentrate on the necessity of really coming one
step nearer that God who had been a reality to him
from childhood, but in relation to whom he still finds
he has left so much undone and unsolved. But he
finds it difficult to reach the necessary degree of concentration, hard to lose himself in prayer, while at
the same time he must prepare for the exacting examinations which have to be passed before he can be
promoted to the highest class of the Gymnasium.
Learning the catechism, as well as all the required
memorisation, seems very irksome and increases the
burden of his work. The notes in the diary which
he now began to keep have therefore at times quite
a gloomy hue. He reproaches himself bitterly for
mistakes he has made, and is also tormented, when
the Fifth Commandment is under discussion in the
Communicants' class, by the thought of how often
he has neglected his beloved mother. The indifference
which often overpowered him as a result of physical

or mental strain seemed to him to be a sin. Nevertheless, he succeeded in fighting his way to a calmer outlook on life. The day before his confirmation he writes: "I believe that the essential thing is to recognise oneself to be a poor sinner, and with joy and thankfulness to receive the forgiveness of Jesus, and that from Him Himself." Both brother and sister were confirmed in the Church of St. Anne in Petersburg. "Our hearts failed us," the young boy writes of the great event. "I had to fight Satan who was trying to make me indifferent, but, thanks to God, my prayer helped me to feel free. What grace I felt in this first partaking of the Sacrament! I hope I shall never forget it! What a joy, what a privilege, to feel Jesus within oneself! One feels completely changed. What goodness and mercy of God that He should give Himself to a poor sinner like me. I must busy myself more with God's word, so that He may busy Himself more with me. I must, with God's help, change for the better lest I should change for the worse." These expressions of joy and gratitude, so natural to a youth brought up in a Christian atmosphere at the time of confirmation and the impressive moments of his first communion, were of far greater significance than usual to young Nicolay. "Jesus within himself" became for him not only the source of joy and peace for his whole life, but also an absolutely binding call to a life of holiness, and a pledge of coming victory—a promise which he had to remind himself of again and again when the battle he waged would otherwise have seemed hopelessly hard. For the inner life of Paul Nicolay in all its simple devotion was never an easy one. He set his goal far too high for that and took into too little account the outside circumstances, which others are so apt to employ as excuses for spiritual laziness. There was no definite "decision for Christ" at the time of confirmation in the life of Baron Nicolay, but this event was just one step nearer that decision, which became finally complete and unreserved after many similar steps through the same battle.

The last year at school, 1879-1880, proved to be especially taxing to the young man's physical strength. Neuralgic headaches, constant insomnia which followed, attacks of malaria and influenza—all these, which were the great trial of his maturer years—he suffered from even during school life, making especially hard for him the intensive study for examinations which formerly marked the end of each term in a Russian school as a time to be dreaded. With his resolute sense of duty, Nicolay now buried himself in his work, but his conscience often smote him when he realised that he could not free himself from that ambition, that desire to distinguish himself which plays a part in every competition. Like a sigh of relief sound, therefore, the words of his diary, dated June 15, 1880: "Finis! I can hardly believe it, it is like a dream. God be praised for having helped me through these seven years of school."

It must have seemed like freedom from an unendurable restraint immediately afterwards to travel abroad with his mother and sister to France, Switzerland and Italy. In France they visited his father's sister, the Abbess Simplicie, in the Convent of Normandy, and also his father's brother Louis at "La Grande Chartreuse," whom Paul Nicolay never neglected to visit in his many subsequent travels in Western Europe. In Italy the family stayed at Lake Maggiore, at Verona, and finally at Venice. Here Paul Nicolay left his family in order to return to St. Petersburg where he was to enter the University. That winter he lived with his uncle and guardian, then Minister of Education, Alexander Nicolay. This stern government official, who considered it every man's duty to serve his country, that is, the State, urged his nephew to study law. As Paul's mother, who had unlimited confidence in the judgment of her brother-in-law, supported him in this, the young man felt obliged to comply with his guardian's wish.

His own interests would have led him in quite a different direction—he loved history, and also geography, astronomy, physics, and other natural and mechanical sciences, in which he later acquired considerable proficiency by his own efforts. Practical activity, and most especially the healthy life at sea, also appealed to him. But jurisprudence with its great demand for dry memory work was, on the contrary, repulsive to him. The first years at the University were therefore almost as hard for him as the last year at the Gymnasium. His health was not improved by his visit abroad, and he felt weaker than ever before. He never used his bad health as an excuse for neglect of study, but he often excused himself because of it from fulfilling the demands which society began to make on the young baron and landowner. During these years he was reserved and shy, and his physical depression brought on a mental despondency, a tendency always to look on the gloomy side, which often seemed to overcome the natural joyousness and good spirits of which, according to the opinion of his young companions, he had a rich supply. In order to strengthen and discipline his rebellious body he began at this time to take lessons in fencing, which exercise was as beneficial to him as the season spent at the health resort in Bavaria in the summer of 1881. During the summer-time he spent a great many hours out-of-doors, devoting himself most enthusiastically to sailing, of which he had been fond from his childhood. In 1883 he purchased the yacht "Lady," which became a faithful friend to him through many a long year. With the pilot Pajuri and one other man as crew, he undertook from Monrepos, where he usually spent the summer, trips to Kotka, Pellinge, Helsingfors, and other places in Finland. In this way he familiarised himself further with the country which was to become still dearer to him, and which, in spite of his Russian upbringing and international connections, he always liked to recognise as his fatherland.

The sailing trips were beneficial to Paul Nicolay both physically and morally. He rejoiced in the manliness instilled in him through the necessity of extricating himself from critical situations, as opposed to the apathetic influences of the life at St. Petersburg. His love for this healthy sport became almost a real passion with him. One of Baron Nicolay's companions of this time says that his desire to acquire true sailor customs would lead him to quite comical

MONREPOS

PAUL NICOLAY AT
THE AGE OF THREE

CALIFORNIA BAPTIST THEOLOGICAL SEMINARY
AUDITORIUM BUILDING
LOS ANGELES 13, CALIFORNIA

exaggerations. He attempted among other things to chew tobacco, and when at night he would turn out the friends who were accompanying him they were forced before going up on deck to swallow a glass of rum, for that was part of the game. The fare on board the "Lady" was of the simplest, coarse bread and dried reindeer steak, so that the guests with more delicate appetites joyfully hailed the first white bread which was offered them on coming ashore.

The out-of-door life at sea certainly helped strengthen Baron Nicolay for the winter's hard battle with jurisprudence. June 7, 1884, he passed his law examination with honours, which like former similar triumphs seemed a marvel to him. "What others attribute to their good luck, I know that I have to thank God for," he writes in his diary. And it was with reliance on this strength that he now attacked his studies for the final examination for his degree.

During this phase of his life Paul Nicolay, in spite of the shyness which had, however, somewhat diminished, as his strength increased, was often drawn into those circles of society where amusements reign. This picture of him as a companion and man of the world which was given by a friend of his youth portrays the young Paul Nicolay in the middle of the eighties, and the circles in which he moved.

"It was a moment rich in significance for me," writes Baron Theodor Brunn, "when one evening at the home of the governor-general, Count F. Heyden, who was living in St. Petersburg at the time, I became acquainted with Paul Nicolay, who was later to become an intimate, well loved, and admired friend. It seems as if it were but yesterday. Miss Olga von Heyden, who became later Lady-in-waiting to the Dowager Empress, came towards me accompanied by a pale thin young man, saying, 'Baron Nicolay, who is also from Finland, wishes to meet you.' I cannot remember what he said at the time, but it was of Finland he spoke, and I had a feeling of gratitude to him for wishing to become acquainted with me. We were both a great deal in society at the time. Paul Nicolay was a good friend and comrade at the University of St. Petersburg, of Alexander Heyden, who later became Flag Officer and Adjutant to the Emperor Nicholas II, but was more intimate with his classmate Dmitri, the youngest of the brothers, who joined the artillery and on retiring became Marshal of the Nobility in Southern Russia. The young people used to gather at the home of the Heydens once a week and played charades. Dmitri Heyden entertained everybody with his jokes. Paul Nicolay was in high spirits, and even if he did not help to amuse the company on a large scale he was well versed in innocent pranks. I remember so well how, happy and boyish, when seated on a Turkish divan in the smoking room beside Dmitri Heyden he said, 'We don't have to say much in order to enjoy ourselves.' And then, experienced as he was in fencing and sailing, he would hit his neighbour a sharp blow on the knee. The latter would try to retaliate, but Paul Nicolay was agile and strong, and with a laugh he was in the other corner of the room. His joy was contagious, for it was so pure and hearty. Alexander Maximovsky, Boris Jakeentschikoff, and Theodor Oom were among the young men of this group at the Heydens'. It was with Oom that Nicolay sailed to Summa and fetched me on board his yacht 'Lady.' They were on their way to visit the Heydens who had rented the artistic home of General von Etter's wife in Haiko for the summer. And it was on this cruise that I received my first impression of Paul Nicolay's very helpful influence on his companions. . . . Both members of the crew, P. & K., were pleasant, devout people who attended prayers, where Nicolay would play for them English hymns on his little organ. But Oom and I were complete heathens. I had lost my faith as a student at Dorpat, and Oom was a cynic and belonged to that class of young people who regarded the creed of the Greek Orthodox Church merely as essential to a position in the world and at court. One warm summer evening we were all three reclining in the cabin while 'Lady' rocked on the quiet sea as on a lake of oil. Oom came out with a shady story or vulgar expression. I seconded him in such language; but, barely had we spoken ere Paul Nicolay urged us in a friendly but decided way to give up such conversation. He was a conscientious and earnest young man in whom we caught a glimpse of the servant of God which was to be. . . . Yes, he could sail, fence, play games, and act, but not as we others did. There was something about the expression of his face which told of a determined fight for the spiritual world."

Paul Nicolay could do everything that those around him did, and yet in doing it he was not like them— this must be the explanation of the deep influence felt even then by his companions. "This young Daniel in a worldly society," as Baron Brunn calls him, never lost sight of the high ideals of Christian manhood. "How I wished that even in the deepest recesses of my soul I might be straightforward, sincere, an enemy of all deceit, industrious, energetic, steadfast but humble—that I might fight and conquer self and without fear of men always let my conscience be the victor!" This we find in his diary of 1882. Even after this he often upbraids himself for idleness, for it seems to his sorrow that he is wasting time. The purity he is striving for is far greater than freedom from merely gross sins. Once when in a moment of weariness he sought diversion in a book which he found to be coarse, he is convinced that reading it was a sin. "What little strength of character I have, that I do not throw away a dirty book in time!" When during the autumn of 1884 in the course of a long journey he visits Paris, he can be seen again fighting against a variety of impressions in order to keep his inner life strong and free from stain. Now, as before, he seeks help in all these battles from the God of his youth, to whom he always bears the relationship of a trusting child. Especially in his sailing trips he accustomed himself to look to God for protection and guidance even in the smallest things, a faith which became a comforting, steadying certainty throughout his life. He was often, as we have seen, depressed by his own inability and worthlessness. These scruples must have been confided to his Uncle Louis when he visited La Grande Chartreuse in 1884, for he writes in his diary how his uncle urged him to trust in God's compassionate and searching love for all his need. The relation between the Carthusian uncle and his nephew, a man of the world, was one of the deepest understanding; and when Paul Nicolay remarks how the conversation turned to the necessity of doing everything for God and not for the praise of men and how they rebuked the cowardice and weakness of the day, we understand that the views of the ascetic monk and the fighting young Daniel must have harmonised in a marvellous way. But Paul Nicolay writes of a cousin de Broglie, also a monk, whom he visited and who grew "less friendly" when he found his Lutheran relative evading the question of conversion to Catholicism. The Roman Catholic doctrines had never appealed to Alexandrine de Broglie's grandson. The worship of saints irritated him who was always acutely sensible of man's nothingness in the sight of God, and once after attending mass he simply jots down laconically, "Glad to have it over." Æsthetic impressions had no attraction for him, but he could appreciate to the full the spiritual greatness of certain Catholics, and the lure of asceticism which one could not fail to notice in his own life must have made him sympathise with certain features of Catholic discipline.

Although the young Paul Nicolay was a pronounced Protestant in his views of life, he could never be termed an Orthodox Lutheran. Lutheran church life of the time was hardly calculated to appeal to a mind as strongly attracted by the essential and practical in religion and indifferent to its historical forms and dogmatic interpretations as was Paul Nicolay's. "Ecclesiasticism" seemed to him even then, as he later expressed it, to be "just as much a party-spirit as any other conceivable form of party-spirit." Even in maturer years he spoke of himself as a "poor denominationalist." Neither did he receive his deepest religious awakenings, except at the time of confirmation, through the church, but rather at home. Baroness Nicolay was devoted to the church of which she was a member, but, as we have seen, her religion worked along other lines than those customary to that church. We have seen how, even from childhood, Paul Nicolay accustomed himself to independent striving towards a personal relationship with God, and when as a man he received a deep and lasting influence from a Christian community, it was not from his native church, but from a society almost unique in its nature and not even recognised as a religious body by the temporal and spiritual authorities of the Czar's Russia. For Paul Nicolay received in the society of the Paschkovites the most powerful impulse to his faith and his first training as a worker in the service of Christ. The Paschkovite movement can be regarded as one of the most remarkable religious occurrences in Russia. It takes its place among the many sects of that country which were built on an evangelical basis. The Russian sects are almost entirely unknown to us. Because the spirit which is, or was, prevalent among so many of them greatly affected Baron Nicolay's spiritual development in the time of his youth, it might be of interest in a work of this nature to describe them in a few words. But, as this would lead too far afield, we must needs confine ourselves to Paschkovism which in many ways resembles the purely popular sects, although of a totally different origin.

The Paschkovite movement originated in aristocratic circles in St. Petersburg. In 1874 Lord Radstock, a leading English evangelist who had spoken in many countries in Europe, came to Russia's capital at the request of a Russian lady of high rank who had heard him speak abroad. Here he held "drawing-room meetings" in many an aristocratic home. Of Lord Radstock Paul Nicolay wrote at his death many years later: "His life was one of wholehearted devotion to his God, and his message was a melody of but a few tones." This man, through his simple talks on the fundamentals of evangelical Christianity, made a deep impression on many members of the Russian nobility. One of those who heard him and were gripped by his message was the Colonel of the Guard, Vasilij Alexandrovitsch Paschkov. In 1876 he filed a request for permission to found a society to encourage the reading of religious and moral literature, and his request was granted. The aim of the society was, according to its statutes, to afford people the opportunity of obtaining at a low price parts of the sacred Scriptures as well as other literature. As a result about 200 pamphlets were published and circulated through the country districts by those appointed for that purpose. Paschkov and those of the same faith —whose only dogma was belief in salvation through the atoning death of Jesus Christ and that this salvation was open to all—gathered in each other's homes for religious meetings. In these gatherings the

numerous servants of the most aristocratic household
and men and women of humble rank were encouraged
to take part.   These meetings were most often held
in the magnificent Paschkovite palace at Nevan, or
in the home of the sisters, Princesses Gagarina and
Lieven, at Bolschaja Morskaja.   Here one could meet
not only pastors but also Colonel Pashkov himself,
Lord Chamberlain Count Korff, and many other members of the new society; and here in the most luxuri-
ously furnished drawing rooms, seated on high antique
chairs of gilt and figured leather, were washerwomen
and farm hands side by side with countesses and
princesses of the bluest blood, often sharing even the
same hymn book—a sight hitherto unknown in Russia.

Tolstoy in his novel "Resurrection" has painted a
satirical picture of this little group.   It is easy to
understand how he who had never looked behind the
scenes saw in it merely a parody of what he called
Christian brotherhood—the outcome of a fashionable
whim or a rising tide of emotion among a few rich
and self-satisfied people.   What the great author
failed to see was the deep, rich peace which "the glad
tidings" brought to the hearts of poor and rich
alike, and which kindled in most of the members of
the Paschkovite society a burning desire for service
and gave them steadfast courage in the face of abuse
and persecution.   It was but natural that the work
of the Paschkovites was very soon to arouse unrest
in the camp of the Orthodox Church.   The Church
publications showered on the heads of these new sectarians abusive words, and demanded their overthrow.
At these meetings no mention was made of saints, of

PAUL NICOLAY AND HIS THREE SISTERS, 1870

the Virgin Mary, or of the Sacraments of the Church, and no icons were found in the meeting places. Was not this sufficient reason for branding the entire movement as immoral and unchristian?

In 1877 an order was issued to Paschkov prohibiting religious meetings, and in the following year the religious authorities were told to urge him and his followers to abandon the error of their ways and return to the fold of the Orthodox Church. As a result Paschkov moved his field of activity to the country places where he could work unnoticed, and especially to his many large estates. In this way the Paschkovite propaganda reached the more distant peoples and came into contact with earlier existing evangelical sects. When Paschkov returned to Petersburg in 1884, he and Count M. Korff called together a joint meeting of representatives of these sects—Stundists, Baptists, Molokans, and others. This meeting was soon forbidden and many of the delegates, mostly peasants from various parts of the country, were arrested, examined, and sent home by the administration. In the same year the society for encouragement of the reading of religious literature was dissolved by governmental ukase. Immediately afterwards the Holy Synod directed the bishops to watch the spread of the Paschkovite movement, and a similar order was given the governors by the Home Secretary. Colonel Paschkov was forced to leave the country and make his home abroad, but the movement continued to spread in the late eighties and through the nineties. During this period it became more and more assimilated with the other existing sects, and grew in many respects more radical and more aggressive against the Church.

But in the highest circles in the capital Paschkovism retained its original character. For here meetings were quietly carried on, occasionally exposed to annoyances from the police but more often, thanks to the protection of the Court, left unmolested. It was here also that Paul Nicolay, in the eighties, first came into touch with the movement. Count Konstantin von der Pahlen, his friend, later to become his brother-in-law, introduced him into the society of the Paschkovites, where his mother also was known, for although she never joined the movement—always remaining a faithful member of the German congregation in Petersburg—she embraced, nevertheless, the spiritual sphere of its activities with warmth and sympathy and had many intimate friends among its members. Paul Nicolay, a student and young functionary, thus came to attend these religious meetings first at the home of Paschkov, whom he did not come to know until several years later, and afterwards at the home of Princess Lieven whose son became a good friend of his. Here he found divine worship simpler and more direct than in the Church, and a much greater demand for personal work on the part of the individual members of the group. The latter had at first an almost terrifying effect on him whose reserved nature shrank from united prayer, and the oft heard sentimentality in the preaching of German and English evangelists frequently repelled him. But there were other aspects of these meetings which must have strongly appealed to him. There was a spirit of earnestness which permeated these people who were striving to serve God in the midst of a godless and superficial world, and it was not rare to meet here those who had borne witness to their faith before princes and rulers and suffered for it in prison or exile. Something of the deep, pure fire of the early Christians must have been rekindled here. And again and again the speeches emphasised complete surrender to the only God as the condition of fitness for use in the service of His Kingdom. It was now made still clearer to the young Nicolay that his Lord might demand a more complete and unlimited possession of him, that an irreproachable life could not be the sole aim of a Christian, for there was *work* for every one who was willing to be used. Gradually this thought ripened within him among this group of Christians, so sure of their faith. "How much spiritual blessing have I not found in the meetings in the home of Princess Lieven," he said to one of his Finnish friends many years later. It was here that the young man often found the needed help for the fight to be able to live in the world without being "of the world." This battle was still far from over in the last years of study, and it was not so to be until he should have found a way out from this "world" into a richer, fuller, and more fruitful life.

CHAPTER III

Years of Consecration

ON returning from his trip abroad in the autumn of
1884, Paul Nicolay writes: "A new phase of life,
a new manner of living is now opening up for me.
I will begin it with God, and pray Him to be with
me and bless me." The new life of which he is thinking is primarily the completion of his studies at the
University and the prospective entering upon his legal
career as a government official. In the winter of
'84-'85 he worked on the thesis for his final examination in law, after the acceptance of which he was
appointed in the spring of '85 to the first department
of the Senate. Some years later he left this civil
service department for the Council of Empire.

But the new work did not interest Baron Nicolay,
and the change from the University life made no great
difference to his habits of living. During these years
his time is divided between the duties of his position,
which he tries to fulfil with his customary minute
conscientiousness, and that life of pleasure which his
standing in society almost required of him. He attends the theatre—which he, not being æsthetically
inclined, does not greatly appreciate—although in his
diary he sometimes expresses enthusiasm over "Faust"
and even mentions the pleasure aroused in him by a
"decent performance" of "Beautiful Helena," or the
thrill with which he watched Coquelin's play. But

his usual remark was, "I don't understand much about it." Sometimes he dances until five o'clock in the morning at the home of friends, and he thoroughly enjoys a party at the home of Grand Duke Vladimir. And occasionally he is also known to have remarked after some entertainment: "I have had a good time" (beaucoup amusé). But in spite of all this he finds time to bury himself in questions concerning a life of faith, many of which become vital to him. His diary thus pictures him pondering over the subject of "Justification by Faith" and over the meaning of the finished work of Jesus Christ. "Can it be true that this work is sufficient for us?" he asks himself in 1884. "What a joy, if it were true!" And in 1885 he writes that he is now convinced of the certainty of Justification, but does not yet understand on what it is based. Of far greater significance than these theoretical meditations is a strong conviction of duty to begin to work for God, and a growing sense of the danger of the worldliness which is trying to make increasing demands on him.

This worldliness had, in reality, very little hold upon his inner life. "Beaucoup amusé" was seldom the comment called forth by one of these so-called pleasurable evenings. On returning from a fancy dress ball he writes: "Never again in my life will I take part in anything like this." Neither is the temptation to ambition and adventure, so common to those of his social standing, of any real danger to him. When during a visit to Helsingfors in 1886 he attends a ball given by Count Heyden for Alexander III, he rejoices to think that he has already retired before the

Emperor, late in the evening, inquired about Baron Nicolay. He even considers it a burden during the visit of a Grand Duke at Monrepos, that same year, when he is obliged to offer his arm to the Grand Duchess Maria Pavlovna, and when on the occasion of a ball a couple of years later he "twice in one round held the hand of the Empress," he remarks ironically that he can now "die in peace." Yet, at the same time, he feels that this "worldliness is robbing him of the spirit of Christ," and the big decision for him during subsequent years becomes: How much of this kind of life is entirely wrong, how much am I entitled to relinquish, for God's sake, not for my own comfort? It is this necessity of taking his stand against the demands of the world, of submitting more fully to the guidance of God's Spirit, which is the new element now entering into Paul Nicolay's life, and which, as his diary shows, characterises most markedly the period from 1884-1891.

Significant of the seriousness with which he attempts to change his habits and remodel his character, is the decision reached in January, 1885, to give up the habit of smoking which had become dear to him. "In order to strengthen my character, with God's help I reached the heroic decision to give up smoking, and have this evening locked away my tobacco and my beloved pipes," is the somewhat humorous remark in his diary. But existence without tobacco while working on his thesis, during the following days, proved to be real torture; he felt a continuous pressure on his chest, was nervous, and out of sorts. It often seemed like pure folly not to put an end to this discomfort by smoking one little cigarette—a remedy certain of success! But when he was about to do this, he recalled "with indignation" that this to him was a forbidden fruit. Later Baron Nicolay often rejoiced over the victory won at that time, for with the years grew his conviction that smoking was a real hindrance to true holiness; "God's Spirit would not approve of it," he often said.

On New Year's Day of the year 1886 Paul Nicolay made two resolutions for the coming year: "not to please yourself," and "never to procrastinate." This year he delivered his first official address in the Senate, and, as in the time of his examinations, he marvelled at the success which so far exceeded his expectations. In spite of the unusually poor condition of his health —being forced to undergo a water cure at Kissingen —he still strove by every means to realise both his resolutions, and to fight the indolence and inclination to idleness with which he, though unjustly, accused himself of being greatly afflicted. Towards the close of the year he joined the society for the relief of the poor of the German Church and visited in this capacity the poor and the sick. He witnessed dreadful scenes of suffering, but reproached himself for being so little affected by them. "Is it tiredness or the presence of another which causes it?" The absence of strong emotions which he was often forced to observe in himself caused him deep concern. It was probably on account of this that in later years he so often emphasised in his addresses that the inner life of a Christian should not be founded on emotions, but on the determination of the will and on the Word

of God.   In his diary of 1887 is reflected the joy with
which he received the words of the evangelist Kargel
at the home of Princess Lieven: "A Christian's duty
is to give himself, not to worry about himself."   He
is also gripped by another picture with which Kargel
illustrates his thought: the strong hand of God takes
hold of man's weak one, all we have to do is to let
Him take hold.   Baron Nicolay often used this illus-
tration in religious addresses.   At a student conference
at Jakobstad it brought release to a student standing
on the borderline of decision, an incident which was
tenderly recalled even after Nicolay's death by those
who were then present.   We may thus realise that the
impressions made on Baron Nicolay in these early
years were deep and decisive, and destined in many a
case to determine the conception of Christianity of his
riper years.

In 1887 Paul Nicolay joined the Russian Bible
Society.   He also participated in the work of the
German Church this year by taking up the collection,
along with other young men, at the services in the
Church of St. Peter.   This must have been to the shy
and, as we know, unecclesiastically minded young
man a great self-denial.

It was at a meeting at the home of Princess Lieven
in January of 1888 that Nicolay for the first time
appeared as a religious speaker.   It was not with
eagerness that he did it, but he did it nevertheless,
driven by a categorical imperative which he himself
describes in the following words: "I was struck by
the thought that if God gives me something to say
I shall be forced to speak, now that the need for

PAUL NICOLAY, 1883

THE FAMILY COAT OF ARMS

speakers is as urgent as it is to-day; that I must learn to get something out of God's Word myself, and not remain a passive pupil merely listening to pastors and others. But it is not for the head to delve out the meanings, but the soul through God, through prayer, as He commands." He already felt a responsibility for the people who have not like him tasted of "the Bread of Life," but are suffering from spiritual starvation, and his one urge was to transpose his faith into action and not to keep the best he possessed for himself alone. A Christian who was not willing to share the wealth of his soul with others he later stamped as an "egotist," an "anomaly." Thus his first appearance at the home of Princess Lieven was not to be the last in that year; the need for speakers was often apparent and Paul Nicolay was always ready on such occasions to fill the breach.

At the end of January of the same year occurred an epoch-making event in Baron Nicolay's life. At that time he journeyed to Helsingfors to take for the first time his seat in Parliament in the House of Nobles as the head of his family. The young Baron's interest in Finland had been considerably augmented during the past few years. When on one occasion, upon receiving a foreign pass, he was called "a Finlander in Russian service," it pleased him immensely. He had begun to study Swedish, and he once gave as an explanation for not taking part in the work of the German Sunday School that he hoped in time to teach Swedish and Finnish children. This interest was greatly increased while in Helsingfors during the session of Parliament. He now became acquainted with many of Finland's outstanding men, was entertained with great hospitality in Finnish homes, and also made many true friends. He became acquainted with Madame af Forselles and her husband Emil af Forselles, also the wife of Colonel Karamsin and many members of the family Wrede, among whom were Professor R. A. Wrede and Miss Mathilda Wrede, and, during the summer, also her elder sister. On a visit to Toivola Home for freed prisoners near the River Kymmene he also met Baron Henrik Wrede, the owner and head of the home, who became one of his best and most devoted friends. In company with Miss Mathilda Wrede he visited Sörnäs prison which he found astonishingly well organised. His attitude toward Finland was especially characterised by an affectionate admiration so often found at that time among "Finlanders in Russian service," which was brought forth on occasional visits to his native land by comparisons between its regulated western ways and the chaotic condition of the great Russian Empire.

Many of these new acquaintances became of great significance to the inner development of Paul Nicolay. He takes part in meetings at the home of the wife of Colonel Karamsin, and with two young men whom he has just learned to know attends free church meetings in the Alliance House in Helsingfors. The attitude to "the world" which was then prevalent among Finnish believers aroused a certain spirit of restlessness in the extremely conscientious young man. We have seen how he still felt it possible to combine religious activity with a worldly life of pleasure, how

he did not consider it right, without great deliberation
and inner certainty, to break entirely with the latter.
Here he comes up against an entirely different point
of view.   Madame af Forselles has described an
occurrence in which this difference became apparent.
One evening the young Baron Nicolay arrived rather
late for a Bible class at the Karamsin home, and without hesitation excused himself on the grounds of
having to be present at a circus given on Broholmen
by society men and women.   At the close of the meeting the young man with the quiet countenance and
questioning look accompanied Madame af Forselles
home, and asked her after a period of silence what
she had meant by the expression "almost a Christian"
which she had used during the course of the evening.
Immediately, almost without a moment's reflection,
came the answer, "Oh, for example, one who goes
straight from a circus to a Bible Class." "The questioning look of the dark eyes became still more
marked," writes Madame af Forselles. "I could
plainly discern it even in the dusky glow of the street
lights, while an almost imperceptible smile spread over
the serious features.   I have never been able to forget
this expression; it appealed to me so strongly with
its complete absence of any trace of wounded pride
or resentment.   What I saw in it was the deep thirst
for truth of a crystal clear character."

Thirst for truth—a sure, personally discovered truth
—can really be traced in the notes in Paul Nicolay's
diary of this time.   He quotes in it Madame af Forselles' thought that he who has truly given himself
to the Lord should no longer love any pleasures, not

even music and similar ones, unless they glorify God. "I could not say Amen to this. Should one live beyond one's understanding (au délà de sa compréhension)?" he asks himself. He prays for clearness in the decision, and some thoughts then come to him: (1) Spiritual growth begins at the moment of our consecration to the Lord; (2) There are different degrees of growth; (3) One should not strive to grow faster than is natural; (4) Jesus alone should be our goal and guide in the spiritual realm, while the opinions of other children of God are of far less (très secondaire) importance. The words in Romans 14:4, "Who art thou that judgest another man's servant? To his own Master he standeth or falleth; yea, he shall be holden up, for God is able to make him stand," now became real to him, and they remained precious to him throughout his life. In the presence of his Lord he tries every truth, weighs every step. When anything begins to seem wrong to his conscience he does not hesitate to brand it as such, but not before. We have already seen how he gave up his beloved pipe and cigarettes. Typical also is his attitude towards the use of strong drink. In his visit to Finland he twice found himself at a party imbibing more than he felt was good for him, and as a result pauses for the first time in front of the temperance question. "Is it right for a Christian to drink more beer than he needs for quenching his thirst?" After a dinner at the hunting club at Nyland where he finds he has not been sufficiently temperate, he begins to consider the adoption of the blue ribbon as the only cure for avoiding anything as humiliating in the future. From an absolutely personal reason and in the same independent way he gives up hunting as a sport. He once happened to shoot a wild duck that was offering her life to save her young, and the question presents itself to the young hunter, how far he "who would have the mind of Christ" can risk committing such an atrocity. Paul Nicolay's reasons at this time are entirely personal, he never formulates any universal principle but considers each individual case; and this method was to remain characteristic of him.

The strongly independent way in which Paul Nicolay considered everything made difficult his position towards much of what his free church friends, with the best of intentions, tried to force him to do. "What is it people on all sides are reiterating to me— that I shall testify and not hide my light under a bushel?" he writes with apparent reluctance. Every utterance of untested emotions, every burst of ecstasy, worked unsympathetically on him. He longs for complete surrender to God, but feels that he can never reach his goal by publicly "giving himself," as he was urged to do, in the Alliance House. This might so easily prove to be but the work of men. The aggressive propaganda methods of others—distributing tracts on trains and steamers, and religious talks with strangers—strongly repel him. But, with his usual conscientiousness, he asks himself whether it is just his weakness and laziness that make him want to shirk. The independent trait in his character is counterbalanced to a certain degree by what has been called "the inclination of an honest nature to choose the hardest simply because it is hard"! When he travels, later in the summer, with a friend to the Caucasus to visit his old uncle he is harassed all the way by self-reproach for not making any attempt to bring spiritual help to his fellow passengers. It seemed impossible for him to *seek* out an opportunity, and he can only with difficulty induce himself to distribute a few tracts when this seemed natural. But this journey which Nicolay in deep remorse pictures in such dark colours came to be of decisive significance to his travelling companion. On one occasion, at a table d'hôte on the steamer, when the latter heard his reticent friend resolutely interrupt a doubtful discourse with the categorical assertion: "This is a sin," it made a deep impression on him and hastened his conversion. Both the friends find themselves on the journey avoiding their fellow travellers, who belonged to a class of people foreign to them. The consciousness of this causes a burning uneasiness in Baron Nicolay. "Have I the holy fire?" Similar doubts were long to trouble him. But his conviction that God has called him to His service grows during this year which was so significant in his life.

He is strengthened in this conviction by intercourse with Christian friends in St. Petersburg. One of these friends now mentioned for the first time in his diary, is a Miss Alexandra Peucker, a talented and warmhearted woman, who gave all her wealth as all her time to work for her Master. Baron Nicolay speaks of her in his diary as "this admirable and fascinating child of God," and he never had reason to change his opinion of her. Miss Peucker, who is still living in Russia where she had to undergo terrible suffering during the Bolshevik régime, is spoken of by all who know her as a soul on fire, a person in whom intensity of feeling, clearness of thought, and great strength of will are blended in harmonious union. In her relations with Baron Nicolay, as with many of his comrades, is corroborated the fact that in isolated cases woman is permitted to play the part of shepherd of the soul of man. The young men often gathered in her home for long and deep discussion of subjects which were on their hearts, and together to delve into the words of the Bible. In December Baron Nicolay met Colonel Paschkov for the first time, and was impressed by him as "a sympathetic man, true, humble and lovable." No greater influence dared Paschkov, soon to be banished from Russia, exert over him.

The complete surrender to God for which Paul Nicolay was striving in these years of consecration, can be considered at the close of the year 1888 to have become an accomplished fact. There was no conversion in the true sense of the word in his life, adjusted as it was from the first to the Christian way of living. But when he, who several months earlier had marvelled over the ability to give up some worldly pleasures, writes in October: "What grace to have been able to break from the world," and when, in spite of all his antipathies, we find him a volunteer teacher in the German Sunday School, we know that the motto of 1886, "Do not please yourself," has become a reality in Paul Nicolay's life. He has now handed over the rudder of his boat to a stronger hand than his own, and has placed himself under a higher command. As he later liked to express it, all that was now left for him to do was to fight; the responsibility of the victory was not his.

He realises full well that Christianity means self-denial. In 1889 he once quotes the English words: "As long as you keep yourself to yourself you can do nothing for anybody," and adds: "This has penetrated into my soul. All these last days I have felt as if my soul were ill and dried up. This evening I asked myself whether I did not still keep just one idol, and I answered no. Then it occurred to me that I had kept one idol—my own convenience [*mes aises*]—and I determined to give that up immediately. *Put the hand of your will on the stone to be rolled away and expect God to do it.* That is why this evening I said to God: 'I have offered up my own convenience as far as I know how, with my will; and I have left the rest to God. *I am willing, make me able.* If only God would add new flights to my life!' " In the same year he writes: "I now pray God every day for the following things which I believe I shall receive: (1) To grow in Him as the branch grows in the vine, and without looking back or in any way breaking loose to grow still more in strength; (2) To adopt the spirit of service for His sake and overcome my terrible fear and reluctance of speaking to others—thus to become a useful servant; (3) That my character may be changed so that I shall not waste my time, but rather gain time; no slackness."

Breaking away from the "world," from the mundane life of pleasure, must, as we understand Baron Nicolay's whole nature, rather have been a relief to him. He was glad of the certainty of not being obliged to submit to the tyranny of society, though at times this changed attitude might lead to conflicts with his environment. In February of 1889 he received an invitation to a court ball to which he had asked his influential uncle, a year before, to obtain him admission. His mother and his eldest sister considered it his duty to accept the invitation, for to decline would be an insult to his uncle who had gone to such trouble to secure it, and lack of respect to Their Majesties. On the tenth of February Paul Nicolay writes concerning it: "It is hard not to see clearly, and to be influenced by my own people. It is only for religious reasons that I have decided to give up the dance. The unpleasantness of being bored and feeling embarrassed I no longer think about, but I feel that God has led me in a definite direction and caused me to abstain from worldliness. To accept the invitation would be to go in the opposite direction, and that might draw me on further." He therefore declines the invitation, realising that he thereby exposes himself to Their Majesties' displeasure and the risk of harming his career as an official. Two years later he finds himself again in a similar position. During a visit to Monrepos, he learned that Czar Alexander and the Czarina were to go ashore at Wiborg on a journey to Langinkoski. "It was immediately clear that Mamma should meet them at the pavilion of the place of landing, but I could not see plainly what I should do. Personally, I would have enjoyed getting a closer view of them and being presented to them, but I did not know what God's will would be since He did not let me attend the court ball. When I prayed to God for guidance I was no longer uneasy. Sunday

morning I opened my Bible at random to the third
chapter of Daniel, and as I read I learned that Daniel's
three friends were not permitted to do all that others
did. Might that have any bearing on my presentation?
But what? Nothing. I go to my room and opening
my New Testament my eyes are attracted to II Cor.
6: 14. 'Allons donc,' I think. Am I prejudiced? At
all events I beseech God to make His will clear and
force me to act in accordance with it even though it
may be contrary to my own. I ask Him to let His will
be done. This evening I will go to the Governor to
hear Count Heyden's opinion about it." Count Heyden
explained that it would be embarrassing to evade his
duty as a subject, and it was therefore decided that
Baron Nicolay should be presented to Their Majesties
along with senators and other men of rank. But that
evening he was struck by the words in I Cor. 7: 17, "As
the Lord hath called every one, so let him walk. . . ."
And these words of the New Testament seemed
strangely significant. All three verses seemed to point
to the same thought, that God "in a very personal way"
could advise a person who was consecrated to Him to
keep away from a worldly act, even when this in itself
implied no direct wrong. In the time which remained
before the day of presentation he could not at first see
clearly what to do, but he felt very keenly that God
really wanted to speak to him through the words of
the Bible, and he was seized "with a great fear of being
disobedient." When on another evening he again
prayed for guidance, he found as an answer the verse
in Acts 16: 7, "The Spirit suffered them not . . ."
"Then I became calm. After having prayed so much

and received such answers, I am convinced that it is God's will, and a restful peace possesses me."

This question which puzzled Baron Nicolay so greatly may have seemed to many unworthy of such serious deliberation, but Paul Nicolay took his whole life seriously, and to one who had grown up in a noble, conservative, and loyal family in close touch with the atmosphere of the court the whole question must have appeared quite differently than to us. The characteristics which Paul Nicolay's arithmetic teacher once ascribed to him and which he himself then spoke of as his only good quality—the inability to leave a problem unsolved or merely half solved—again makes its appearance. His problems were, for the most part, ethical in nature, and throughout his entire life there loomed up before him a series of important and difficult tasks, all of which with God's help had to be solved.

During the years following his consecration, "in a very personal way" Paul Nicolay is guided into that fellowship with God which he had chosen to be his part. In 1889 he was taken very ill, and the thought of death with all its seriousness forced itself upon him. In spite of the pain he suffered he felt that God was very good who would thus prepare him. "Fear not, but believe." As the fever diminished, life seemed like something new, as a gift, and he prayed that his consecration might be more complete and that all he did in the future "might be tested by the spirit of death." He now began to take part in the evangelistic meetings for Germans conducted in St. Petersburg by the Christian bookseller Grote, and assisted him with the after-meetings for those who wished to come into personal fellowship with believers. In his own home also he arranged similar meetings. On July 14, 1890, he journeyed to England to attend a "meeting for the deepening of the spiritual life" which was held annually at Keswick. On this trip he also visited the church of the famous evangelist Spurgeon and became acquainted with Lord Radstock and his son, and many other outstanding Christians. Even before the start of the conference did Nicolay feel that he was facing a big and decisive event and jotted down in his diary the significant words: "I am consecrating myself," and on another occasion: "I am renewing my covenant with Jesus Christ." He was honestly striving to free his faith from all emotionalism, "for so should faith be." "All the time I believe in Christ with my will," he writes in his characteristic way. The atmosphere of spirituality and peace of the Keswick conference impressed him deeply. It became more evident than ever to him that his peace rested entirely on God and His will and did not depend on his own feelings. The certainty of the granting of one's petition is not necessary when one prays, but only the assurance that God hears—is a thought that brings comfort to his struggling soul. With his whole heart he desires God to equip him for His service, and he prays for "a new standard of prayer, a new standard of faith."

CHAPTER IV

First Seeds Sown

AS it became clear to Paul Nicolay that he could and must give up everything which merely served his own pleasure, he began to consider whether he ought not to sell his idol, the yacht "Lady." He even advertised it for sale, but as no prospective purchaser appeared he abandoned for the time all plans for disposing of it. But Baron Henrik Wrede made a suggestion to which Nicolay after some hesitation agreed. Why might not "Lady" be used in the service of the Lord, as a Mission boat? For there are among the rocks and islands girding the coast many districts where it was seldom, if ever, that a sermon could be heard, and where it was almost impossible for the inhabitants to procure a Bible or any other good book. Baron Wrede offered to accompany his friend on his first trip, and in the beginning of August, 1890, they set forth.

The two friends went from Toivola, where Baron Nicolay had been visiting, to Kotka where "Lady" lay at anchor in the harbour. From Kotka their course led to Suur-Musta, where they spent a day distributing tracts to friendly folk of the island coast. Baron Wrede spoke to the people and read to them a Finnish sermon, which his friend at this time was unable to do on account of his deficient knowledge of the Finnish language. On the following morning they continued their journey under a strong gale to Majasaari and Nuokka and from there to Aspö. Half way across a great thunder storm arose from the direction of Aspö, frightening Baron Wrede, who was a poor sailor and was already beginning to feel the effects of seasickness. He therefore begged his friend to turn back as soon as possible and put him ashore at Fredrikshamn. Baron Nicolay did this and returned to Monrepos, grateful for having seen how this new work should be carried on.

But there still remained one great obstacle in the way of this work, the language. If Baron Nicolay was to travel alone this obstacle became almost insurmountable, for as yet he had but an imperfect mastery of Swedish and knew very little Finnish. With renewed energy he immediately began to take lessons in Finnish so as to learn enough to enable him at least to sell books. He was greatly encouraged when a member of the Russian Bible Society offered him four thousand Finnish tracts, and seemed to see in this a sign of God's approval of his project. On July 14, 1891, he considered himself ready to undertake his second missionary journey. He went first to Swedish speaking districts where he could more easily come into touch with the people, landing first at Orrengrund where he met with a friendly reception from the pilots, and from there visiting Boistö, Reimarslandet, Kampuslandet, and Kungshamn. Baron Nicolay often left the shaping of his course to wind and weather, believing that Christ, who was Lord even over them, through them would give him the needed guidance. He had not yet formed any definite plan for the work itself, and he was often undecided as to how to attack it. How his work took shape can best be seen from detailed descriptions he himself left as a record of the first missionary cruises. In their simple reality they bring to us a true picture of the Baron tract-distributor on board his yacht and in the often difficult and thankless work ashore. Some excerpts from his English diary which he kept during his first journey may therefore prove to be of great interest.[1]

"A boat from Kungshamn comes with milk and berries as a present for yesterday's tracts! Weighed anchor. Saw a lot of men a little further at work, drawing timber out of the water. Anchored again, and went amongst them giving tracts and speaking as well as I could. With one man had a nice, close, pointed conversation. They bought several New Testaments in Swedish and Finnish and were very nice. Then, after hesitating where to go, dared to go up an unknown way through Parlaksfjärd. Stopped and visited V. D-berg village. Men out hay making and women at home without money. In one house saw a poor sick young tailor's wife, gave tracts and a New Testament. Why couldn't I pray with the sick woman and make her well? In many places they beg me to wait, while they cook coffee for me; but no time. . . . Would to God I knew better how to speak to the people, more to the point, and that I should be in such communion with Him as to hear His voice every time I speak. . . . Fine morning, light southeast wind, heavy air. Rowed ashore with Pajuri

---

[1] Quoted from English Diary.

and went to the village. About sixteen houses. Mostly women. Spoke Finnish. Some seemed touched, gladly accepted tracts, but didn't buy a single book. They all of them have a New Testament and most of them Bibles, too. While the men are away the women may not spend any money. Prayed before entering a house. Spoke mostly about God's peace. 'They that have not Christ's spirit are not His.'—Rom. 8. 'Christ's spirit, spirit of peace,— have you got it?' Always the same evasive answer: 'We ought to have it.' Sailed to Kaunissaari. Went to the pilot house, met there three men. One seemed almost ironical, another listened. They had no Bible nor New Testament, and didn't want them; had them at home. Everywhere these confounded sermon books, asking after Psalm books, song books, sermon books. Went across the island about 3 km.—hot weather, heavy bag. Met one nice man making hay. He asked me into his house and gave me coffee. God bless him. Most people out, sold but one Bible, people not very encouraging; may the tracts do their errand. Near a boat five or six people were gathered. When I began they met me with a smile, but got very serious at the words, 'peace with God,' and so I could deliver a message. Returned on board and sailed. Thunder clouds to windward, got their wind from the south and came in beautifully to Kotka. . . . On board you always must look sharp, it possesses you, and I lose the living communion with God. Yet God consoled me in His own loving way. This morning I opened my Swedish Bible to Isaiah 44, and my eyes fell on the words underlined: 'Du ar min tjänare, du varder ej av mig för-

gäten.' [1] That was for me like a message direct from
the King. God has acknowledged me as His servant
and reminds me Himself that He is not forgetting me.
How precious I treasure this message and thank my
Lord and Master for it."

We can well understand how this inexperienced missionary felt the need of encouragement and help in this
his first really hard task. He is conscious of how exceedingly little he can accomplish through his distribution of tracts and the words he may speak. But he feels,
nevertheless, that duty calls him to continue on the way
which God has directed. When he comes up against
obstacles, either of an outer or inner nature, he often
wonders whether it may not be a sign of his having in
some way displeased his Lord and forfeited His confidence, by carelessness, indifference, or disobedience.
This thought troubles him, "as in former years," and
shyness and self-criticism once more make their voices
heard calling him away from the hard task. But at
such times he finds comfort in the conviction that God
loves him in spite of everything, and throws himself
with renewed energy into his work. About a town
whose inhabitants still seemed "discouraging, lifeless
and indifferent," he writes the significant phrase:
"Well, the seed is at least sown." This thought gives
him courage.

He described in his diary the way in which his conversation with the people often shaped itself. The
only regret is that since this was written in English
the answers of these island folk lose some of their
original freshness. The details are very character-

[1] "Thou art my servant . . . thou shalt not be forgotten of me."

istic of Baron Nicolay's way of going to work at this time. A typical conversation follows : [1] " 'The Lord Jesus Christ bless this house.' Sometimes, 'Thank you,' sometimes—no answer. 'Good morning. I've brought you Bibles and Testaments, have you got any?' 'Yes, we have a Bible, several Testaments and lots of books.' 'That's very nice—and have you also got peace with God?' 'One ought to have.' 'Have you prayer and sermon books?' 'No, only the Word of God.' 'Remember we won't live long, the Lord Jesus will very soon return or else He may soon call us away. We must be ready to meet Him.' 'Yes, our life is very short on earth.' 'Well, he who has peace with God has everything, and he who has not has nothing, although he may be a very learned man. God will give you this peace, if you will only accept Him. Read John 1 : 11-12. Have you accepted Him? He loves you and wants to save you.' "

They were very simple words which Paul Nicolay, with his limited knowledge of the language and his lack of practice in speaking to peasants, could bring to these isolated people. But they often bore fruit. Many years later he spoke with good-natured irony of his early attempts as a country evangelist; but what may seem to be a failure does not always prove to be one. Full often the inhabitants of these islands or rocky coasts wondered at the frail gentleman with the bulky bag of books, at his abrupt questions and the foreign accent of his speech, but even that wonder paused before what he had to say. The honest convincing tone,

[1] Quoted from the English Diary kept by Baron Nicolay at this time.

the "earnest questioning look," already familiar to the
reader, also possibly the knowledge itself that expressing words of admonition was not easy to him who
said them—all this made his unaffected, unskilful sermon truly worth while. What self-denial all this "aggressiveness" must have cost him with his naturally retiring disposition! He often writes during his missionary trips that he has not the least desire to speak. But
characteristic of him is the striking reply he once jotted
down after such a confession: "It doesn't matter."
After inviting the people to remain for a talk on the
Bible which he was to give that evening, he remarks
that it seemed like "an invitation to his own funeral."

The work among these rugged peoples to which he
devoted himself through so many years became, at
least, of educational value to the man who was to become "a fisher of men" and an extensive organiser.
Above all, this work broadened the range of his experience. On these trips he met people of the most
varying types—Hihulites behind whose severe legalism
he succeeds in detecting a breath of life, self-sufficient
followers of Hedberg who seek him out merely for
discussion, Russian fishermen who expound to him
their theory that Jesus' work of salvation availed only
for those already dead at the time of Christ, and not
for those now living, who must secure their salvation
through their own works. He gradually learns to
adapt his teaching to the individual circumstances of
his audience. "Spiritual hunger," he finds, "must first
be aroused before it can be satisfied." He fixes his attention on the individuals who make up the mass, and
begins to find the right words when as shepherd of

souls he has to deal with personal sorrow and anguish.
Thus a troubled mother is comforted by the story of
Augustine, the son of tears. Men with soul hunger
seek him out on his journeys, and he is often summoned to beds of illness.

Through all this grows his faith in the grace of God
which alone can enable him to be of spiritual service
to his fellowmen. "To look up to God, that alone gives
strength," he writes in 1893. "We could do nought
but let Him work." In the midst of toil and hardships
he finds time for a personal communion with God, a
communion whose depth and beauty far surpass the
usual measure. The life at sea often fills him, the lover
of the sea, with a deep, pure joy. He loves the times
when the sea is sky blue and the rocky island coast is
beautiful—"the Mediterranean and Capri," he once
wrote on arriving at Hogland—but also rejoices in
"angry green waves capped with white," in a fresh
breeze and a good sail. But in all this he sees above
all his God. He seeks to learn and follow His will
whenever he plans any undertaking at sea. "Pajuri is
often nervous about our marvellous manœuvres," he
once remarked. He always asks his Lord to take
charge of everything and exclaims on seeing his prayers answered: "How good of God!" His ability to
trace the hand of God in the smallest things—characteristic of him through life—was greatly augmented by
these cruises. It is a child-like, impulsive, happy thankfulness which, in 1895, after an experience of faith,
exclaims: "There is no such thing as chance for God's
child, but such a coincidence is a little gift, a little
token of the divine goodness." Still nearer his God is

he brought in the hour of danger, and several times on his journeys does he have a narrow escape from death. But closest to his Maker does he come when at times he would go to Him alone, not in prayer nor in songs of praise, but with great yearnings and devotion. Around such moments the simple words of his diary create an atmosphere of holy silence that we dare not break.

The nature of Baron Nicolay's work was virtually changed in the year 1893. He was no longer content to distribute books and work through private conversations and occasional Bible talks, but took with him on board his yacht one or more evangelists, mostly Finnish speaking, with whose help he was able to arrange for larger meetings on the various little islands. Among these preachers were Mäkinen, Soikkeli, Saarinen, and Skutnabb. Even these helpers did Baron Nicolay receive, as it were, straight from the hand of God. He prayed, before starting on a cruise, that only those men who were driven by an inner impulse to take part in the work should present themselves, and he was convinced that his prayer was heard. As a rule he was pleased with his companions and delighted with their simple, straightforward teaching. In the following years sailing trips were taken to other parts of Wiborg's island coast (Björkö, Püsaari, Pitkäpaasi) as well as to many places already visited. Many a time was their course steered to Hogland and islands to the south and east of this island, such as Tytterskär and Lavansaari. The meetings were usually of an entirely improvised nature, for there was no time for extensive preparation.

Baron Karl August Wrede has described the method of procedure on one of Nicolay's missionary trips in which he took part, to an island outside of Fredrikshamn. The news was quickly spread that a meeting was to be held at a stated hour for adults, and one a little later for children. Baron Wrede inquired whether he was expected to speak at the meetings. "Yes, if you have something you would like to say," responded Baron Nicolay. "How is the program arranged, in what order will things occur?" his guest continued to ask. "That is of no consequence. God will show us that." This method of arranging a meeting seemed somewhat strange to Baron Wrede, who was, however, soon convinced both that the meetings would be well attended, and the evangelists have ample opportunity for personal talks with many on "the one thing needful." Baron Nicolay did not feel excused by the assistance of the evangelists from any obligation of speaking himself. It was here that he became accustomed to giving religious talks in Swedish, and he even occasionally spoke in Finnish when that seemed necessary. But he did not gain any greater confidence in his own ability: "How useless I am as an evangelist, how hard it is for me to be aggressive," he wrote even as late as 1896 from Hogland. Yet he never left an opportunity unused. In many places he laboured with the Salvation Army, with which he had already become acquainted in the work at Wiborg. At first he was displeased with some of their methods, but he did not feel justified on those grounds in turning away from an organization whose work he had to recognise as self-sacrificing and fruitful. "One should never be too decided in one's first antipathies," he wrote, after expressing his aversion to public witness bearing.

One form of work, which he started during his first missionary year and which he had to perform entirely alone, was the selling of Russian New Testaments and devotional books on the warships stationed near Trångsund. He usually had no difficulty in obtaining permission to go on board these ships, and it was very seldom that his request met with a decisive "ne nado" (not wanted). The sailors were gathered together on the deck, gazing inquisitively at the books which were being exhibited. On some ships they were very eager to buy; one sailor, for instance, turned to another with deep disapproval and said: "What kind of a sailor are you not to own a New Testament!" But it also happened that they would laugh and regard the books and the vendor merely as a curiosity. The attitude of the officers depended entirely on whether they knew who the quiet and unpretentious salesman was. After being treated with aloofness on one ship where he was forced to exhibit his wares on the floor of the deck, he might on the next be invited to the officers' quarters and received as a baron. "I feel like a Cinderella," he writes after such an experience. It was a temptation to him, when visiting the ships of the Navy, to reveal at once who he was and in the company of the officers to make his appearance as a man of the world and not as a missionary. "It makes you feel as if in another world. You have the desire to be there in the pleasant rôle of a visitor, and not on the pathway of God." He had so many interests in common with these officers, old acquaintances in St. Petersburg, politics, and above all, yachting and the Navy, his passion. But to converse on these things when he had come on board on the commission of God seemed to him like wasting time and avoiding possible discomfort and annoyance. His honest nature also revolted against any appearance of disloyalty to the cause he served. This along with the wholly foreign atmosphere of the Russian warships made this form of work very difficult for him, but he felt called to it and did not give it up as long as his mission along the island coast lasted.

Thus the idea of converting his "idol" into an instrument in the service of the highest things of life was brought into fulfilment. The summer months were no longer a time of rest for Baron Nicolay, except when with reluctance he was compelled to go abroad because of his state of health. These months on the contrary became times of intense strain and fatigue. He could feel so tired that "his body would hardly hold together," but the work filled him with a rich joy. "The end of a cruise is often more blessed than its beginning," he writes on one occasion. His joy reaches its height when at times he is permitted to see that his work is needed in many places, and that it is even bearing fruit. He mentions a "meeting which was blessed" at Kaunissaari where no pastor nor layman had preached for three years, and at Tytterskär he meets a person who found peace with God after his visit of the previous year. He loves his yacht with a new and hallowed feeling, and must still occasionally ask himself if his delight in yachting itself may not play too great a part in his life. But those are but passing sentiments, and in 1897 he writes: "I am sure that there will be a picture of my yacht in heaven, for thus has God known how to utilise my idol." Yet the thought of selling the yacht, of giving up this mission to the island coast, comes to him more repeatedly at the close of the 1890's, and in 1901 the thought is realised. The reason for this must be found in the many new duties which were now making a claim on him, so that he does not consider it right to spend large sums of money on a boat which he would now so seldom be able to use in the service of his Master.

Baron Nicolay's Christian work in the nineties was not limited to his missionary cruises along the coast in the summertime. During the autumn and winter months in St. Petersburg he sought to utilise every opportunity of coming into touch with spiritually hungry men, of winning souls for Christ. He distributed Gospels in hospitals and spoke to the patients; and he was always eager to enter into conversation with cab drivers who frequently drove him through the city, seeking to interest them in the cause of the salvation of souls—often succeeding, as this thought was not foreign to the ordinary Russian—and giving them tracts and copies of the New Testament. The "isvostschiks" were certainly grateful to be treated as if they were of value as people, and not merely as a means of conveyance, in the eyes of a gentleman. Baron Nicolay mentions with joy in his diary how a coachman, whom he had once talked to, recognised him several years later and told him of his conversion.

In the year 1897 Baron Nicolay began regularly to gather around him a group of young men, probably members of the German Y. M. C. A., with whom he studied the Bible and whom he tried to interest in home missions. In these years he addressed various societies, such as the German and Finnish Temperance Societies in St. Petersburg, and often spoke at the home of Princess Lieven. Speaking he found just as difficult as during his journeys along the rocky island coast, but the inner compulsion to share with others the treasures of the Christian life mastered him. His attitude at that time made speaking especially difficult, for he believed that the subject for an address should never be chosen "by the mind" but "by the means of prayer," through the working of God's spirit. Consequently, he often found himself on the platform not knowing on what subject to speak. But he always found guidance, although this might not be until the eleventh hour. For unprepared in the true sense of the word he never was when he came to a meeting; while searching for a theme he had delved into many texts, and one thought had usually matured and been clarified, although at the time he was not certain if this were the right one for his address. In the address itself he often suffered from an inability to free himself from thinking about people, and could not speak as if in the presence of God. He sought for the cause of this weakness in his "spiritual undernourishment," and decided, with the words of the Psalmist, "Seek my face," daily to set aside half an hour more than formerly for private meditation and prayer.

In the meantime a larger and infinitely harder piece of work was beginning in 1896 to make the first demand on his time and strength. That was the work which, until the year 1905, he was to carry out in the numerous overcrowded prisons of Russia. It was with the German-born evangelist, Baedeker, whose home was in England and who in 1875 at the request of the International Bible Society first visited Russian prisons, that Paul Nicolay became acquainted with this work. His admiration of Mathilda Wrede's work in Finland, which he had been able to see at close hand—including a visit to Kakola prison in 1888—and the enthusiasm with which she spoke of her work, helped to arouse his interest in the cause. Baedeker, who did not want to limit himself to distributing Bibles but also wished to talk to the prisoners, knew no Russian, and so it was in the capacity of interpreter that Baron Nicolay, who had by now mastered many languages, accompanied him in the winter of 1896 to prisons in St. Petersburg and Moscow. In the following year he undertook an independent tour to many other towns—Novgorod, Staraja, Russa, Tver, Bjeschetsk, Rschev, Vjasma, Rybinsk. And in the succeeding years he extended his journeys to a great many new places, using for this purpose not only his longer vacations but also every occasional holiday from his work. These trips were extremely taxing to the health of the physically weak young man. The close air of the railroad compartments, the crowds at the stations, everything, tired him. Yet the journey itself was not always the hardest part of his task. To arrive some autumn evening at a miserable country place half drowned in deep, dark mud, to be jolted along in a rickety cart over the poorly paved or entirely unpaved road, to be finally harboured in a dirty hotel room where the much needed sleep became an impossibility, could be far worse. To Paul Nicolay, who, in spite of his ascetic nature, was used to a relatively large amount of comfort, these rooms became a virtual source of dread. But neither this nor anything else could keep him from travelling; hardships, on the contrary, always spurred him on to renewed efforts. After a more or less sleepless night it was necessary for him in the morning, with aching head and often shivering with ague, to call on the prison director of the town and relate to him his errand. When Baron Nicolay had already obtained permission to visit the prisons for the purpose of distributing Bibles the directors were usually very obliging, often regarding him as a sort of official sent by "higher authority" to the prison. On one occasion a prison director greeted him in official tone with the report: "All is well." When all the formalities were over the prison doors were opened to him, and the day's work began. This work consisted primarily in giving out Bibles to the prisoners, and Baron Nicolay was supplied with Bibles in all the languages spoken within the Russian Empire—Russian, German, Polish, Esthonian, Lettish, Armenian, and others, including Swedish and Finnish. Occasionally he was permitted to accompany the prison keeper from cell to cell thrusting books through the doors to the individual prisoners. At other times all the inmates were assembled in the prison chapel where the books were distributed and where Baron Nicolay was usually allowed to give a religious address. The effect of the concentrated and apparently impenetrable mass of misery and crime which this audience represented often nearly overcame the speaker, who had to exert himself in order to look these unfortunate people in the face. The need was so vast, and what he could do to relieve it was so extremely little. Only the thought of "the strength which is made perfect in weakness" brought back courage to carry out his purpose in spite of the consciousness of his own impotence.

Paul Nicolay had the advantage over Baedeker in his complete mastery of the Russian language, by means of which he could easily make himself understood to most of the prisoners. They were words of comfort which he sought to bring these unfortunate men: "You are not under the wrath of God, but under the tears of Christ. If Christ in dying for you has done the greater, shall he not also do the less—forgive, receive, help?" He often spoke of the power of Christ to save and restore, especially of His power to save from the Russian scourge, drunkenness. This made a deeper impression on his audience than all else. A young man once fell at his feet when at the close of such an address the speaker handed him a copy of the New Testament, and a Lettish prisoner wept for joy on receiving a copy of the New Testament in his own language. But the audience was not always in such a sympathetic frame of mind. Sometimes the men would talk and laugh aloud during the address in spite of the rigid discipline, trying to create a racket which forced Baron Nicolay to strain his weak voice in order to make himself heard. How distressing it must have seemed thus only from a distance to be able to talk to these indifferent or hostile-minded men, whom there was neither time nor opportunity to win, and how hard while journeying to the next town to recall a few faces which stood out from the mass and impressed themselves on the memory of the evangelist as pictures of grief and sin. Neither were there always books enough to go round, and he was forced to let some of those he wished to serve turn empty-handed away. And the dirt, the misery, of these overcrowded Russian prisons—is it surprising that Paul Nicolay after coming from one of them simply jots down the words: "Dead tired!" Especially at the start of a missionary tour does he often feel broken in body and soul, and not until later comes the strength which accompanies every self-sacrificing work. "I feel so refreshed after a prison tour, just as if I was inhaling deep breaths of fresh air, and I am often full of gratitude to God for the great privilege which is granted me," he writes on December 8, 1898, of a feeling which often recurs to him.

How indefatigable Baron Nicolay was in his labours is best shown simply by enumerating the towns, merely in European Russia, which he visited between 1896 and 1905. Besides places already mentioned are Schuja, Kineschma, Luga, Porchov, Pskov, Ostrov, Jamburg, Vyschnij, Volotschok, Vladimir, Valdaj, Torschok, Jaroslavl, Vologda, Rostov, Alexandrov and Arkangelsk. Most of these places were visited several times. In 1901 he also undertook a journey to the famous and frightful prisons of Siberia. His diary gives us a detailed account of this trip. The last day of May Baron Nicolay left Petrograd, spending one day in Moscow, and then continuing to Nischnij Novgorod where he visited two prisons. The description of these visits is characteristic. "Things would not go well at first. I realised that I must hurry and that the ground was hard. It was head work and lacking in spirituality. As I drove to the other prison I prayed the whole time that I might be filled with the Holy Spirit, and now things began to take on a new and vital turn, praise be to God!" Later he visited other prisons along the Volga and its tributaries, among them Kazan where Baron Nicolay was able to give his Tartar driver an "Ingil" (Gospel) in his own language, also Sarapul, Ochansk, Perm, and Vjatka. In Jekaterinburg, the last town passed in European Russia, he met the evangelist Kargel who was to accompany him to Tobolsk. From Tjumen, a small place on the Asiatic side, they continued the journey by boat. Baron Nicolay studied the many interesting types of people on board, especially the Tartars of Central Asia. In Tobolsk work began anew. But it was not until later, on the trip up the Irtysch River, that he first came into touch with true Siberians. He writes of a town through which he passed: "Five high wooden crosses rose from the church yard pointing towards Heaven. Here Poles are buried, banished without doubt. Many believers have even been banished to the district of I-ska. The thought of this ill-fated country, these places of exile, and the misery of those who were sentenced to live here as if buried alive and forced to end their days in such wretched holes, makes one shudder." Near Omsk he discovered a Finnish colony whose minister, Pastor Eriksson, invited him to be present at the dedication of a new school house where he had the opportunity of speaking to the colony in Finnish, thus utilising the ability to express himself in that language which he had acquired on his sailing trips. "We ate, and we drank coffee as in Finland," he remarks of his visit to Helsinki. In Tomsk, where Baron Nicolay arrived on the 5th of July, he passed from one overcrowded prison to another. In one of them he found 657 prisoners whom he could only see by going from cell to cell. "It went all right in the beginning when I waited on the Lord, but afterwards I became too tired," he writes in his diary. "Gave away 350 Russian books, about 12 Yiddish, 8 Esthonian, 2 Lettish, and one Finnish." Krasnojarsk, near Yenisei, the first spot from which the mountains could be seen, was more encouraging to the traveller. Here he distributed 990 books, one of the pastors of the town being sympathetic and helpful, and the coachman who drove Baron Nicolay thanked him more for the New Testament he gave him than for his pay. Yenisei is described in the diary as a magnificent river. From Irkutsk Paul Nicolay writes: "I feel that I have learned on this journey always to believe, although there may not be any visible proof, that I have all things in Christ, and to act accordingly. To-day in the prison I realised so strongly that God alone is the completion of God's work, and things went better than usual, thanks be to God." Transbajkal, Verhneudinsk and Tschita were the last stopping places on the journey. In all these towns he continued the difficult and apparently almost unfruitful work with the same faithfulness, the same quiet confidence that "God was sufficient for His work," and full of gratitude to God who by holding His protecting hand over him acknowledged him as His servant. From Tschita, on the 25th day of July, Baron Nicolay

started on the long return trip. He reached home on the
5th of August, and four days later was at Stockholm
on his way to a Northern Student Conference. The
fact that he had suffered from malaria on the boat trips
in Siberia and that his strength was almost gone on
reaching home—that was of no consequence to him
when it was a case of following a programme of work
previously planned. How like the words of St. Paul
in the Second Epistle to the Corinthians (11 : 26, 27),
"In journeys oft . . . in weariness and painful-
ness. . . ."

In the summer of 1899 Baron Nicolay asked for permission to resign from the department of State. This
was granted him in November of the same year. His
interest in the duties of his position had not increased
in the course of the years, but rather diminished as
his desire to work for Christ gained control over him.
The knowledge that he could not work as the others,
that he could never concentrate his thoughts on the
work itself, troubled this conscientious man, who also
felt that his health was being impaired by the divided
attention of his life. Neither did he feel that the moral
influence he might exert on a few companions by remaining in their midst was of sufficient importance to
make this his duty. The good friends he had made in
the Senate and Department of State would not be lost
by his resignation. His best friend in this official circle
was Alexander Maximovsky, whom he had learned to
know and love in his University days. Maximovsky, a
highly talented man equipped with a great capacity for
work and juridical sharp-sightedness, later became

head of the Russian prison administration in which capacity he strove, as far as lay in his power, to realise the Christian principles which had become his. Even after the paths of the two friends had drifted apart, their friendship remained unchanged.

Another factor influencing Paul Nicolay's decision to give up his position in 1899 was the prospect of work for the Student Christian Movement, which that year was opening up for him. But as another chapter will be devoted to this, his great life work, we will merely touch on the incident here.

This chapter has sought to deal with Nicolay's work during a period of about ten years. Although he threw himself into this work with self-abandonment and enthusiasm, it was natural that he could not perform it without occasionally resting. It was often necessary for him, greatly against his will, to care for his tired body. He suffered frequently from influenza and malaria, two diseases which it was almost impossible to fight successfully in the damp climate of St. Petersburg or on his strenuous journeys. Neither was Monrepos climatically suited as a place of residence for its owner, who once exclaimed with a touch of bitterness: "Why have I not a home in which I can live!" He was at times forced to yield to the demands of his physician and seek a cure abroad; thus visits to health resorts came to play an important part in his life. He was never an ideal patient concentrating his attention on the care of his health and the observance of rules. But these times of enforced rest seemed hard to the arduous worker, who, however, used them as times of intensive spiritual growth when thoughts might mature and the will be strengthened for the fight. To realise this fully we must accompany him on a couple of the journeys he was forced to undertake for his health.

After an unusually severe attack of influenza he left, in August 1894, for Kneipp's Sanatorium in Wörishofen in Bavaria. On arriving there, "after half a minute's examination" he is prescribed for, and he begins the life of a guest at the sanatorium, conscientiously complying with the regulations. But his diary reflects deep inner struggles and a burning desire, at least by personal testimony, here also to serve his Master's cause. He seeks out among the other patients "des compatriotes du ciel," and he is troubled by the worldliness he finds in those around him. When he finds it still hard for him to make the attack, he asks himself to what this lack of love for souls, as he calls it, can really be traced. Had not the destruction of the unconverted soul yet become a reality to him? Would it not be better to make the "charge" himself than merely to approach with open visor? His inability to utilise opportunities for "personal work" often distresses him. "In books one always answers correctly, but I often do not know what I ought to say," he writes on this subject. "If the opportunity to speak presents itself, I have not the desire; if I have the desire no opportunity presents itself." He asks himself how he ought to make the attack, and as usual he can not rid himself of the question until he has sounded its depths.

Again and again the solution of the problem floated before him, as he in time would definitely come to grasp it. "You should pray for the opportunity, not seek it—not as I will, but as God wills. No initiative on one's own part is necessary. All that is necessary is to live close to God and let oneself be led by Him. A Christian ought to be like a display in a shop window, all the merchandise must be plainly shown so that no explanation is needed." His characteristic sensitiveness and honesty kept him from overdoing the "witnessing" which the Anglo-Saxon custom in this respect might have led to. Only his old suspicion of "convenient" solutions forced him again and again to reconsider the problem. In his intercourse with the other patients he also sought to make use of every opportunity of helping them to Christ, certainly without coercing them in any way, he who had to force himself to aggressiveness. Some examples might be of interest. A Pole at the Sanatorium interests him, and he seeks his companionship. On a walk the man falls to his knees before a crucifix by the side of the road, and this naturally leads to an unsought-for conversation about sacred things. The Pole was friendly, but hardly receptive, and Paul Nicolay writes a few days later: "If I can not show him anything else, I can at least show him sympathy, affection." Another time it is a wealthy English-speaking lady who awakens his interest. She evades every conversation on religious subjects, the reason for which soon becomes apparent as she is a Jewess. Later she becomes more willing to talk, and informs him that she is a Unitarian. "What shall I do, I have no arguments," writes Nicolay in discouragement. His inability to argue on religious questions forces him to seek to clarify the basis of his faith which, on account of his being more ethically than intellectually minded and the course which his evangelistic work hitherto had taken, he had possibly too much neglected. His main argument, after serious testing, becomes one which he willingly cited later in his work among students: "If Jesus is not the Son of God, then the main theme of the Bible is a fake." He uses this as a weapon and rejoices in its success, but later learns what makes the greatest impression on others is not his argument but his own immovable and sincere faith. One who was wholehearted in that faith could never fail to attract honest seekers. "How important it is to be an instrument in the hand of God; I am led along an individual road and only need to follow my guide." These comforting words were Paul Nicolay's expression of the joyful experience he had.

From Wörishofen Baron Nicolay journeyed to Salzburg where he visited Colonel Paschkov for whom the gates of Russia were now barred, and from there to Switzerland where he called on old Samuel Zeller in Männedorf near the Lake of Zurich. Männedorf has been described as a place "where people come who are afflicted with all kinds of diseases, people broken in body or soul, people who are melancholy or mentally deranged, people who have not found peace with God, and also people who are only physically ill—and people who seek a peaceful spot where mind and thoughts can find that quietness they crave, and where new strength can be found to work anew, if God so wills." [1] On all the sick who so desired, and on those alone, Zeller laid his hands in prayer for them, and many claimed to have regained their health there. Zeller, who also sought to help the patients by means of a

[1] Hans Koch: "Agnes Rothe."

healthy régime of life as well as by prayer and Bible readings, in which his powerful religious personality is brought to the fore, made a very favorable impression on Baron Nicolay. Gentleness, strength and wisdom, as well as practical ability and cheerfulness, attracted him to this unique man. "It is a joy to hear him pray." The visit to Männedorf brought refreshment to both body and soul.

Baron Nicolay speaks of the following year as a "time of spiritual testing and poor health." But whatever his difficulties at this time may have been, he was better equipped than ever before to face them. He could therefore remark that he "stuck it out and squeezed through." His strength lies in the assurance that Jesus is in him and he in Jesus, and never for an instant does he lose hold of the thought that "Jesus *for* me covers the past, Jesus *in* me supplies all needs of the present." He sees still clearer that Jesus' work is far bigger and wider than we can now have any conception of; what we may know of it now is merely a glimpse of the greatest. In the beginning of the year 1896 he writes that he is again giving himself over to God as a slave—simply as a slave. We recall that this was the year in which he began his work in the prisons. But his poor health necessitated his going abroad again at the end of September to Adelboden in Switzerland, where he spends some weeks. Here the old problem of "testifying" faces him anew, but, as before, he comes to the correct conclusion: all that is needful is "to walk hand in hand with God throughout the day, to enter into it in the guidance of the Holy Spirit." In Adelboden he attended several religious meetings, including a "Meeting of the Brethren," to which people came from many different directions and the spirit of which greatly impressed him. A trip to Hauptweil followed, a place of rest for tired Christian workers where he was at first "bored," for he had nothing to do and to listen to many addresses during the day he found too strenuous. But intercourse with Stockmayer, the director of the institution, and one of the nurses, Schwester Emilie, brought him much that was worth while, and when he leaves Hauptweil he remarks that he has here learned how much he still has to learn. Stockmayer's parting words: "We are going towards the same goal, guided and protected," are long echoed in his soul.

The friends Baron Nicolay made on his foreign journeys and the impressions he received abroad became of great import to his spiritual development. Of all the countries visited during his lifetime—and that life could be called one long pilgrim journey—none made as deep an impression on him or became as dear to him as England, "dear old England," as he nearly always calls it in his letters, and which he often longed for during the later years of his life. The English language and English customs he had become familiar with even in the nursery. His sisters and he had been cared for by an English nurse, and English had, in compliance with the old family traditions, along with German been the language spoken in the home. He had in his youth through the Paschkovites also learned to know and appreciate the Anglo-Saxon form of religion. A strong feeling of spiritual fellowship always filled him in his intercourse with English friends.

This feeling was greatly strengthened during his visit to England in the autumn of 1897, when he visited many old friends—Dr. Baedeker in Weston-super-Mare, Mr. and Mrs. Penn-Lewis and Mr. Sloan, the deputy director of the China Inland Mission living in Bromley, near London, whose whole family he was very fond of and with whom he corresponded up to the time of his death. He took part, on this trip, in a conference at Cambridge, after which he journeyed to France where he no longer had that same feeling of being at home. For Paris and the Parisians he has only words of disapproval; he gets a painful impression here of moral decadence. He feels quite foreign to the relatives he visits in France on this occasion.

Towards the close of the year 1897 and during the first months of the following year Baron Nicolay suffered more than usual from attacks of fever and malaria. When no cure or medical treatment seemed to avail he began to wonder whether he ought not to refrain entirely from all human expedients, and seek his cure from God alone. A visit from Baedeker, who claimed to hold views expressed in the last chapter of the Epistle of James, strengthened this belief, and he now made several attempts, after prayer for healing, entirely to ignore his illness; to "receive in faith" the cure whose coming was delayed. It seemed so hard never to use more than "half the engine," not to be able to give all that he wished, and it was such a humiliation to his strong faith that he was powerless to pray his way through this weakness. Each time a cure proved to be a failure, each time the symptoms of malaria made their appearance on the journey home from the sanatorium, the disappointment he experienced was equally keen. Prolonged experience, as well as talks with Mr. Sloan and Dr. Hudson Taylor, the well-known Missionary to China, who came to visit him in St. Petersburg, gradually led him to the conclusion that the use of remedies was justified even if it was only for a time that it alleviated suffering, the complete cure of which was evidently not according to God's will. "God is always right," he would say to drive off the feeling of disappointment, and he taught himself to see that "the best way to bear trials was to accept them." The fact that his illness forced him to spend so much time on himself was especially trying to him. He was troubled by the enforced idleness. "Can God permit such an *easy life* as mine?" he asks himself. The words seem like a paradox in face of the great burden of work he was carrying at this time, but they were spoken in all seriousness. Complete self-abnegation always seemed to Paul Nicolay to be the Christian's aim; we recall his "giving up one's own convenience" at the time of his consecration. "My motto will be *selfishness with a cross over it*," [1] he writes with a characteristic turn of the pen. The belittling of self seemed to him the first condition of a fruitful life; selfishness brings its own punishment—unfruitfulness. His exhortation to himself one New Year sounds like a cry for perfection in the fulfilment of duties. "Be friendly, friendly, friendly! If possible never defer the performing of a duty. Never let time be wasted. Duty first; duty, cost what it may. Be always true in all things." His craving for self-renunciation reaches its height in the fol-

[1] Quoted from Paul Nicolay's English diary.

lowing: "When one renounces self, one ought also to renounce all dreaming and thinking where self plays a part." This bespeaks battle, and there is much to show that these years were times of trying experiences, of difficult inner struggles to Paul Nicolay. In 1899 he was stricken with a bitter sorrow, and it may be the echo of this which reverberates in these lines written in spite of his severe judgment of his dreams: "I have like most people had a beautiful hope, but God has not realised it." But the backward look was not allowed to influence the course of life. Paul Nicolay has learned to look ahead where things were waiting to be done, and close upon the sad words follows the courageous decision: "I therefore want the ambition of my life to be to glorify God in speech and self-sacrifice." These words were written in 1899 when Baron Nicolay was about to "give up everything" and enter upon a new field of labour where the harvest was plenteous and the labourers none. He was now to find the task, which he alone was called to perform—work among young people who were thirsting for truth, who were, during the remainder of his life, to mean more to him than brother and sister, father and mother, or worldly goods, and in whose service he would utilise all that he himself had gained through personal seeking and personal strife.

CHAPTER V

Among Russia's Students

IN the spring of 1899 Dr. John R. Mott, General
Secretary of the World's Student Christian Federation, and Dr. Karl Fries, its Swedish Chairman, came
to Helsingfors, where a group of students within the
Y. M. C. A. purposed to organise an independent Student Christian Movement. Baron Nicolay was invited to take part in the conference where this was
to be discussed, and he was also asked if it would be
advisable for Dr. Mott to go to St. Petersburg also, to
speak about the work of the Student Christian Movement and possibly lay the foundation for a similar
work in Russia. Baron Nicolay replied that it would
not be a complete impossibility, and stressed the fact
that the low moral tone and the spiritual need of the
student world of Russia urged an attempt to reach
them. The letter ended with the words: "We can
promise you no meetings, but Russia is the land of possibilities, as some one said, and it is worth while trying. Come and see for yourself what can be done.
We will continue in prayer."

In April Baron Nicolay met both of the student
leaders in Helsingfors. He was greatly impressed by
the personality of the energetic American with his
strong faith—"genuine, unaffected, calm," is his comment on Dr. Mott; and he became deeply interested in

this work with which he was now brought into touch for the first time. The aim of this work—to make Christ King among the students of the whole world—must have appealed to such a mind as his. When Dr. Mott went from Helsingfors to St. Petersburg to see for himself "what could be done," Baron Nicolay went with him and remained as his assistant and guide. They were unable to arrange for public meetings, but in St. Petersburg as in Dorpat and Riga, where Dr. Mott made short visits, he was able to address smaller groups.

It was one evening at the home of Princess Lieven, where the foreign visitor was telling of the work of the World's Student Christian Federation, that became decisive for the future course of Paul Nicolay's life. During the address it occurred to him, that possibly the man whom God should call to organise a Christian Movement among Russia's students might be among the audience in that very room. He glanced from one to another of those present, but he found no one whom he could picture as a leader of such a work. And then with dread he was forced to ask himself: "Could I be the man? Has God allowed me to grow up, study, and work in this country among Greek-Orthodox companions, has He allowed me to become familiar with the Russian language and customs, and given me besides an evangelical home and contact with Christians of Western Europe, to prepare me rather than all others for *this* task?" Thus approximately must the question have come to him, and the answer had to be an unconditional "Yes." Paul Nicolay had trained himself to obey higher orders, and he now laid the hand of his will to the new plough. Many times were doubts of his own ability for the position to steal over him, threatening to overpower him, but he would not take his hand from the plough until it should be forcibly torn from his grasp.

The students of Russia! Although there was a great deal to prove how especially equipped to serve them Paul Nicolay was, it must be admitted that there was almost equally much to prove the opposite. What prospect in the work itself could this half-foreign Baron with his puritanically tempered religiousness, his reticent and reserved demeanour, and his Western European outlook on life, have of approaching this mass of vibrating nerves, hungry intellects, and surging chaotic emotions, which is, or rather was, called the studying youth of Russia?

He had received his education and his scientific training in Russian schools, but as one of his closest relatives, Baron A. Meyendorff, puts it, he had "passed through the Russian 'gymnasium' and the Russian law school with evident aversion although with remarkable conscientiousness." Hardly a single expression of the Russian mind, be it in art, science, or public life, continues Meyendorff, had taken root in him, save only the essentially democratic conception of life and the indifference to conventionalities which characterised him. He never really lived the life of a student. What could he know, except through books or by hearsay, of the cold attic or cellar room where a student shivered over the borrowed book and sought warmth through a glass of often unsweetened tea, or argued into the small hours of the night about modern social, philosophical, or ethical theories with companions as threadbare as the host himself? He had not eaten scanty meals in cheap student restaurants, nor run long distances through the capital in search of poorly paid tutorial positions; nor, above all, ever had the police close at his heels. Never in his youth had he been the least bit revolutionary, but, on the contrary, belonged to a class which shrugged its shoulders at the "Nihilists." No, he had never been a Russian student in the true sense. One reason for his so seldom coming into contact with those of his fellow students who were not born into his social position was the political oppression, as a result of which it was almost impossible for anything official in national or social life to be questioned.

Illuminating to Paul Nicolay's relation to these fellow students is an entry in his diary of 1882. He is telling of a comrade who visited him and played chess with him. They entered into conversation in which his companion shows himself to be a man "of character and strong principles." And he continues: "Maybe through him I could get to know students of the *simpler, poorer, but industrious and honest class.* This would evidently mean breaking from my old habits, but perhaps it might be for my own best." Pride it certainly was not which formed the gulf between young Nicolay and his companions of the "simpler, poorer class," for that trait was entirely foreign to his straightforward, unpretentious nature. One of his colleagues in the Imperial Senate tells that what he can best remember of Paul Nicolay from the time they were together is his severe criticism of a companion whom he found to be conceited. This trait continued to be repulsive to him in every form. The cause of the chasm separating him from the mass of the Russian student world must, if external conditions be disregarded, be sought in a different side of his character and outlook on life. His outlook on life was, even in its religiousness, to a great extent "matter-of-fact," thoroughly sober and practical. It might be said, probably with a slight exaggeration, that ideas were realised by him only in that measure in which they could be applied to life; words to him were significant primarily as the forerunners of action. The less real and less effective must, in accordance with his views, always be subjected to the more genuine; consequently the æsthetic and intellectual must give way to the religious which leads more directly to God—in his eyes the only great reality. He who held such a view could hardly be attracted by the Russian intellectuals' vague and often impassioned ideals, their lack of moral and physical discipline, and their rationalism. Their finest traits of character—their impulsive cordiality and freedom from criticism of other people, and the unlimited capacity for devotion to an ideal—often found expression in ways which could not attract him, who was primarily a man of will power. And the faults which predominated among the Russian intellectuals were of the nature which he was least inclined to judge mildly. Thus there arose a breach between him and the people whom in 1899 he felt called to serve. Six years earlier, when he had once felt called to address a group of fifteen Russian students and follow it with a discussion, he had been conscious of not knowing how to treat "these young rationalists." And yet there was a power which should be able to break down all barriers between him and Russian students. It was the great "love for souls" for which he so often prayed and which, unknown to him, burned within him forcing him along paths which of his own free will he would never have chosen.

Great need—soul need—prevailed among "these young rationalists." The religious and moral conditions of the educated Russians presented, as a rule, a pathetic picture. To the Greek-Orthodox students the idea of a personal religion was usually unknown. Most of the students who came from country districts or from less highly educated homes in the larger towns, maintained during their years of study a sort of secret fondness for the ceremonies of the church which were familiar from childhood; others a dim religiousness tinted with mysticism; while an occasional one really preserved his childhood's faith as a vital power. Most of them turned with indifference and scorn away from the Orthodox Church, whose clergy, by their narrow-minded dogmatism, or, more often, their personal indolence and lack of idealism, repelled young people. Those students who came from homes of priests were themselves often the greatest haters of priests. And when the national church was weighed in the balance and found wanting most of them were ready to have no more dealings with any form of religion. The existence of God might possibly be discussed from a philosophical point of view, but, with the new century, the materialistic theories were still so popular that even this was unusual. To be religious was usually considered synonymous with being reactionary—the worst thing possible in the eyes of the Russian youth—and the empty space left by religion was gradually filled by politics. Socialistic and anarchistic theories became to most of these young men their religion. They spoke of "revolutionary ethics," "the revolutionary conscience," which were often widely different not only from Christianity's higher conception of ethics and conscience, but also from what usually goes by that name from the ordinary human point of view. This mirage of a revolution became a Moloch to which youth, strength, personal safety, and life itself were brought as an offering. It was at least an ideal. But although this rising flame of revolutionary idealism did lead its followers to Siberia or to the gallows, it often happened that it died down with the first glow of youth only to leave behind a pile of burned out ashes. That weariness of life and melancholy, which Tschehoff expresses so vividly in his novels, or at least a dull tedium which created the need for losing one's self in the crowd to become "like the others," replaced the lost enthusiasm. And they became like the others, entered into the trivialities of everyday life, lied and were gay like them, sometimes like them under the influence of drink, or in a time of uproar voiced their wail of woe against society and existence. For it was not they themselves, but rather "the cursed system" and "our unfortunate Russian nature" which was to blame for everything, as had been proved in the time of her world wars. That much and hardly more; for when a man's faith in the only ideal served by his mind and soul, namely the revolution, is lost, he usually loses hold of all other ideals, simply "throwing the child out with the bath water." And it must be admitted that "the cursed system" was such as could break the moral stamina of many a pure but weak nature who lacked the support of a firm foundation or hallowed traditions. The doors to all kinds of lawful social and political activities were closed, officials and representatives of free professions lived generally in economic distress, flaring were the injustices of the social order, and the gulf between the great mass of the people and the "intellectuals" so great as to encourage in the latter a feeling of isolation and lack of foundation. All this created an unhealthy and depressing atmosphere, a spirit of weariness of life which came to even the youngest. Many passed through their revolutionary period as "gymnasiasts" and entered the University free from all illusion, with merely the deep desire for more enjoyment than ever before. Many never came as far, but were overcome by the pain and sorrow of the world, succumbed to despair over unsatisfactory examination results, and put an end to their lives. There was need, deep soul need.

Baron Nicolay was not ignorant of these conditions. He had noticed among his associates in the Senate and Parliament dishonesty and laziness in otherwise amiable men, and in the prisons he had laid eyes on prodigals who had known better days but were dragged down by fatal circumstances which they were powerless to combat. He had seen noble natures go astray, which with care could have developed to their full beauty, gaining a new and fuller value of life in a disconsolate world. Others answered the question, "What can bring Help?" with a change of government, a constitution, a democratising of society, more culture. To Paul Nicolay the reply was entirely different. Past the externals he looked into the heart of the matter: no system could avail if it lacked the people to support it. Offer an ill person the most delicious food and he turns away from it or eats it to his own destruction; but cure him first and then he can benefit by even the coarsest bread. What Russia needed, as Nicolay saw it, was the renewing of the whole individual by a living ideal and an imperishable hope, the vital power which comes through intercourse with Jesus Christ, the Savior of life. This consciousness helped him across the gulf which separated him from the Russian students, and for their sake he became one of them—"Greek among Greeks," wrote one who had watched him in the work. "All things to all men that he might by all means save some." When later at the conference of the World's Student Christian Federation he described the life of the Russian student, the terrible loneliness, the unwholesome living conditions, the moral indecision, he spoke no longer as an outsider, for he had lived and suffered and loved his way into what he depicted.

After Dr. Mott's departure Baron Nicolay began in his quiet, faithful way, without any vast plans for the future, to make use of the impulses which his visit had called forth. In the latter part of the summer, while visiting abroad, he carried on an eager correspondence with some of the leaders and workers of the World's Student Christian Federation, among others with the German Missionary, Witt. It was necessary first to secure foreign speakers willing to speak at St. Petersburg and possibly also at other Russian cities during the ensuing year. As we know, Baron Nicolay had already sent in to the government his resignation at the close of that summer's missionary journey and before his trip abroad. This was granted on the twelfth of November, from which date he was free to devote himself to his new task. But he did not immediately give up his missionary work in the prisons. Not until 1905 did he give up that work, and then reluctantly, forced by the steadily increasing burden of his labour in the service of the students.

Mr. Witt came to St. Petersburg in November to deliver a series of addresses for German students, and during his visit a group of those interested in the Student Christian Movement met for an advisory meeting in the home of the bookdealer Grote. This meeting took place November 18, 1899, which day thus became the birthday of the Russian Student Movement. Those who were then present were, besides Baron Nicolay, Witt, Grote and one of his friends, four German students and one of Polish origin, a member of a Roman Catholic family, though himself a Protestant. This man had been led to a personal faith through reading one of Moody's books which he discovered in a little second-hand bookstore. They met to discuss the possibilities and ways of the work; no more was as yet conceivable. But nevertheless it seemed a great and important event. Baron Nicolay wrote about it in his diary: "We expect God to lead us step by step, and we feel the significance of this beginning, since from a grain of mustard seed it may develop into a big tree. How important to begin aright!"

A very small beginning, a veritable grain of mustard

seed, the first year's activity among students proved to be. By political and religious compulsion their hands were bound. They could not hope to reach large crowds with the evangelistic message but had to fight for permission even to talk to a small group. It was to the Protestant students alone they could turn in the beginning, gathering them together for Bible study and inviting them to the addresses of the foreign speakers, Witt, Hartwig, Baedeker. The larger gatherings were held in the hall of the Lutheran City Mission. But not even here could they meet without difficulty, for the Lutheran pastor, accustomed to annoyances from the authorities and also rather suspicious of the new movement's sectarian aims, at first proved to be moderately hostile. Baron Nicolay explained with difficulty that he was "neither for nor against any church, but only *for God against sin.*" Gradually the pastor's doubts were dispelled, and he was even willing to take part in the work, although still urging the obtaining of proper police permission and that the work should, for safety, be considered as a branch of the German Y. M. C. A.

Once a week the students met in the home of Baron Nicolay for Bible Study under his or the Pastor's leadership. The number attending these meetings fluctuated greatly and was never large; even in the second year of the work there were usually only three or four students who attended. Baron Nicolay saw clearly from the first that the movement must begin with the winning of a few individuals, but nevertheless it was discouraging to see how few he was able to reach, especially as he did not succeed during the first years in leading any members of the Bible group to a real decision for Christ. The Pole, Mr. S., was for long the only converted one among the young men.

In the spring of 1900 Baron Nicolay was greatly encouraged in his work by the invitations he was able to accept to student conferences in many countries, a Finnish one at Åbo, a German one at Eisenach, and an international one at Versailles. On his being invited to the latter two he wrote to Dr. Mott:[1] "Your proposal to come to the conference at Versailles was a surprise, but as I hope to be at Keswick in July I will do what I can to be at Versailles on the 4th of August. May the Lord's will be done in this matter. I should like to go to Eisenach on the 9th of August. There is no work to which I feel myself so much drawn and for which I would be glad to devote my life as just the Lord's work amongst students. But as yet I have no conclusive indications of His calling me into it and therefore I remain somewhat reserved, waiting for the Master's orders, whatever they may be. John 3 : 27."[2]

Baron Nicolay was very happy to feel that he was wanted at the Åbo Conference. Although his work among Finland's students will be taken up more fully later, it might be of interest here, as he stands on the threshold of his career as a student leader, to mention some of his impressions of the conference at Åbo and his contribution to it. Both are characteristic of his conception of the work he was about to undertake. He was delighted to find at Åbo over "150 people, mostly students, both men and women, gathered for such a purpose," but he had certain objections to the organisa-

[1] Quoted from the original English letter.
[2] "A man can receive nothing except it be given him from heaven."

tion of the conference. In the first place he was dissatisfied with the name "Student Conference with a Christian Programme." Not only the programme, but the whole conference should be Christian. He also wished that future student conferences might last at least four days, and not as now a little more than two; the programme could not be condensed into so short a time. At present there was "too much preaching, little rest, little spirituality"—time was needed for prayer meetings and private interviews in order to dissolve and absorb what had been heard. At least one evening should be set aside for an "aftermeeting" and private talks with the students, for the "net should be drawn in, the iron forged while it is hot." The public should not be permitted to attend the meetings, whose addresses should primarily bear on the needs of the students present, for the public intruded and gave a superficial atmosphere and took up room.

His conception of the problems confronting the student work at this time, when he is still hesitantly asking himself whether God has a place for him in this work, is significant. But especially characteristic of him is his striving for depth, sincerity and spirituality in Christian work. This is apparent in all his proposals. Such striving was even evident in his speeches, in his contributions to discussions, and it was already plain that he would in time occupy a prominent place in the Student Movement of Finland.

Baron Nicolay went, as he had planned, from Keswick to attend the conference at Versailles. Although his health was very poor at the time of the conference, he felt that he was richly benefited by the interesting reports of the delegates from the different nations. He was especially impressed by the appeal of the representative from China, which brought him for the first time into touch with the Christianity of the Far East. He remained merely a listener and observer on this occasion.

At Eisenach, the next conference he attended, he felt far less at home. He considered that many of the addresses were "lengthy and far too scientific," and despondently asked himself why he had come. But he soon made many worth-while friends, and his first feeling of being ill at ease was to a certain extent overcome. He was invited to speak on the Russian work, and had the opportunity to secure speakers for Russia. From Eisenach he went to Blankenburg to attend an alliance meeting, and from there to Davos for rest and, as usual, to seek a cure for the persistent malaria. Here he stayed in a villa most of whose occupants were Englishmen, and he thoroughly enjoyed hearing and speaking English and the intercourse with English people. He rejoiced especially in his fellowship with Dr. Hudson Taylor, whom he had long known and admired and whose simple, lovable, and childlike prayer-life strongly appealed to him. Here he had also the opportunity of meeting Mr. Sloan and travelling with him to Zurich, where the change of air was immediately felt in the further impairment of Baron Nicolay's health. But again, as formerly, he received strength to ignore his physical weakness. The work was waiting for him; even in Davos he had reproached himself for his inactivity, and "felt his spiritual weapons being blunted," and had undertaken, though a patient himself, to visit the sick in evangelistic work. He was, to be sure, possessed by a certain dread of St. Petersburg, that city of malaria, but if he was not to return who would take up the work for the Russian Student Christian Movement? He realised that he must not, at least for the present, abandon the post where he had been placed by the Master.

On his return he took up the work with renewed energy, following about the same lines as in the preceding year. Every Friday the students met for Bible study, and in order to incite them to self-activity and arouse their power for reasoning, Baron Nicolay sometimes let them choose the subjects for discussion. He also urged them to keep "the Morning Watch," by which he meant, as Dr. Mott expressed it, that they should begin each day with a quiet time alone in the presence of God for Bible reading and prayer. When foreign speakers visited St. Petersburg printed invitations were sent to a great number of students, Protestants only, but it was a great event if an audience of fifty actually came to the meetings. On one occasion, when Dr. Hartwig of Germany spoke, only thirty-five out of four hundred and fifty who were invited came. Five *new* students at a Bible class was considered remarkable, and worthy to be noted, and this in great St. Petersburg with its many institutions of learning and vast masses of students. One evening a solitary student made his appearance. Baron Nicolay writes concerning it, that he was at first discouraged, but that even that "meeting" did not prove to be entirely fruitless. Simply to send the young man home had evidently never occurred to him.

Publicly announced meetings for larger student audiences could as yet not be arranged, for the police as well as the authorities of the Lutheran Church proved to be anything but accommodating. A great deal of faith was certainly needed in order to endure throughout these early beginnings. New openings must continually be sought for, and Paul Nicolay sought and gradually found them, not with "his head" alone but also through the intuition of love and communion with his God. He wrote that he felt all difficulties were fundamentally derived from "the opposition of the unseen hostile force." In his teaching he maintained that all things should be "from God, through Him, and for Him." But he also gradually familiarised himself more with what might be called the technique of the work, acquiring the habit of meeting "student arguments," although he was averse to learned discussions and always tried to foster the spirit of "simplicity and devotion" at his Bible talks. He persevered, and it was soon evident that his labours had not been in vain.

In 1902 there was a marked change for the better; a new spirit of seriousness and devotion seemed to grip the student members of the Movement, and there were evidences of real conversions among them. Baron Nicolay now wrote that for the second time in his life he felt *as if a great victory had been won in the unseen world.* It was now that the first really Russian Greek Orthodox students joined their numbers, making it possible during the early spring to hold a Russian meeting every other week. "It is growing" was the leader's joyful and confident reflection on the work. In March the first conference was held for all the members of the Bible groups, and when autumn came there was such a large majority of Russian student members that it was decided from now on to have all the meetings conducted in Russian, a language familiar also to the German members. Thus Baron Nicolay could say of the Student Movement in Russia, at the conference of the World's Student Christian Federation in Sorö in 1903, that the "flickering wick had not been extinguished," and also that "a nucleus was being formed which possessed real life." He rejoiced more over this nucleus of men with a living Christian faith than over all other successes, for he saw plainly that "Bible groups and other outward forms might lack spiritual life and thus become a building without a foundation, an organisation without conversion."

The students who now comprised the nucleus of the Movement had been won through his unceasing vigilance over the flickering wick of their souls, by participating in their moral difficulties while setting a high standard for them. "The aim of all our meetings is to lead souls to Christ, to complete conversion," he once writes. And conversion he characterises thus : "To me it implies a genuine breaking away from all known sin, a surrendering of the complete personality to Christ." He was convinced that God always worked from the inside out, and that the Student Christian Movement would degenerate and die out if it did not in reality lead souls to Christ. To fortify the members of this "inner circle" against their temptations was now to become his main task, nor was this always to be an easy one.

In spite of changed conditions the obstacles in the way of the work were many and often caused Baron Nicolay deep concern. He speaks in his diary about the students' incapacity for independent work and the difficulty of having to combine German and Russian students with their different temperaments within the same groups. Many a time he is still subject to despondency, as when in the spring of 1903 during a serious illness he learns from his doctor that he is suffering from the early stages of hardening of the arteries. Death seems very close to him, and he sorrowfully reflects, "If I should die now, God would certainly have accomplished very little through me." For the sake of his people and the Russian Student Movement he wanted to be allowed to live yet a while longer. For although he at times still wonders whether he be the right man to lead this Movement, he feels responsible for its development. During his convalescence at Davos he is busy translating into Russian for his students Dr. Mott's book, "Individual Work for Individuals," and on his return to St. Petersburg he finds tasks of great importance awaiting him.

Baron Nicolay discovers to his joy that "it works." He is now able to arrange for two kinds of meetings regularly, for larger audiences and smaller groups for the Christian students. The meetings of the first variety were not attended by religiously minded students alone, but also by earnest doubters with whom Baron Nicolay had long private talks. In the Bible studies on the great personalities of the Old Testament, which were held for a smaller group, the students, heretofore usually passive, now begin to express themselves, contributing of their own religious experiences. It is a joy to the leader to hear a testimony like the following: "I can't help believing," from a young man who but a short time ago had said: "I can not believe," and to see the changed expression in his face which had before told of a dull hopelessness. A recent convert confesses that he had nearly committed suicide, the usual resource of the discouraged Russian student: "I lived without God, and life had lost its significance for me, and I wanted to do away with my life; but now I have found God." Baron Nicolay describes this student as "talented, thoughtful, energetic, and kind-hearted," and it was such a young life which came near being thrown away. What a joy to see him saved and happy!

Gradually the "nucleus" is growing. When Mr. Robert Wilder, one of the outstanding men of the Student Christian Movement, visited St. Petersburg in 1904, the number of believing students who wished to meet him was as high as twenty, and the Movement continues to reach more students. A foundation is laid for the work in Riga and Dorpat. When Paul Nicolay reflects on his own oft-recurring faintheartedness he feels deeply impressed by the goodness of God.

In 1903 an important branch of the Student Movement came into existence, when its sphere of activity was extended to the women students—"kursistki." It was in this year that Miss Ruth Rouse, woman secretary of the World's Federation, visited the capital of Russia. A very small group of women students, only ten, came to hear her at the home of Baroness Nicolay. Later they met at that of Miss Peucher, who undertook to organise this group. Quicker and richer than the work among the men was the development of this newly organised work; the inherent religiousness, the conscious or unconscious thirst for God was more marked among the women than the men students. The loneliness of student life was harder for them to endure, and the moral anarchy, which held sway in the circles where many of them were forced to move, became more quickly unbearable to the young girl than to the young man. Scientific materialism was, to be sure, most enthusiastically embraced by many "kursistki," but to them it was largely a matter of fashion, seldom being based on deep study or mature conviction. When life through it became dark and empty, when suicide began to seem the only solution of the mournful problem of existence, then these naturally emotional and warm-hearted young girls reached forth eagerly for the new set of values which was being offered them.

A Russian student has told of what an overwhelming impression the new light in which Christianity was revealed by the Student Movement made on many of her companions. It was the message of a *living* God which gripped them irresistibly as an entirely new conception. They might even have attended church and called themselves Christians, but to "think of God as living—how glorious and yet how terrifying." To feel themselves face to face with the Great One who had seemed infinitely removed from them by reason of His very holiness, became an experience naturally followed by the need of a personal Savior. Thus the way was paved for evangelical teaching. And it was but seldom that this teaching led the young women away from the church of their fathers; as a rule they felt that they had simply gained a new and more intimate understanding of the *significance* of her ritual, and a new longing to serve her as true Christians.

Through the young girls who were won, the influence of the Student Movement penetrated more deeply into the homes than through the young men. Significant is the story of a student who came from a clerical family, among whom she was the only one who believed in God. When asked if she did not dread returning to such a home, she replied: "No, they know at home what I believe, and they envy me."

Miss Peucher continued to be the leader of the branch of the work for women, founded in 1904, until the year 1907, when it was taken over by Miss Marie Bréchet. But, as some phases of the work were common to that among the men, Paul Nicolay became virtually also its leader, and the work continued to develop along the same lines as the original Student Movement.

When at the close of the year 1902 the Movement began to expand, Baron Nicolay realised the need for a stronger organisation of the inner circle which formed its nucleus, in order that the character of the work and the terms for membership might be independent of circumstances. In 1903 he suggested that the various Bible groups select "elders" ("starosty") to lead them, and in the same year he presented to the members of the inner circle a "basis"—in reality a short confession of faith—for membership in the Student Christian Movement. But there was a good deal of delay before the question of a basis was finally settled, as the declaration in its original form did not meet with approval and had to be worked over many times during the ensuing years.

The discussions on the subject were often of a rather violent nature. Students, and especially Russian students, are seldom inclined to state their views of life in definite terms by adopting any kind of formula—and they sought to give to their basis as extensive and vague a wording as possible. Neither was it Paul Nicolay's intention to force the Student Movement into any dogmatic strait-jacket, but he felt keenly that it needed a backbone, that the movement must be made up of people ready also to confess with their mouths what their hearts believed and having a perfectly clear conception of their relation to Christ. He therefore wished to frame the declaration so that no one could sign it without at the same time taking his stand as a Christian. In the beginning of 1905 a unanimous decision was finally reached on the question, and on February 5th fifteen students in St. Petersburg signed the following basis:

"On the basis of the Gospel I believe on the Lord Jesus Christ, the Son of God, have experienced a change and given myself to the Lord, and know that He has received me."

Thus the active membership was now, as was also to be the case in the future, limited to a relatively small group which, however, became, as Paul Nicolay so much desired, the force from which power and warmth were radiated throughout the Student Christian Movement of the entire country.

It is amazing to note the great progress made by the Movement in this trying and restless period for Russia politically, the period of the Japanese War and of the first Revolution. A less favourable soil for the spreading of religious propaganda among students, whose interest in politics must have become more absorbing than ever before, can hardly be conceived of. And this obstacle was felt, but it was also overcome.

Paul Nicolay himself was by no means an indifferent observer of what was going on. The war had from the start aroused in him a feeling of deep concern. "It is pure folly of Russia to begin war," he writes in his diary. Prophetically full of forebodings he foresees the coming calamities. Right before the great catastrophe of Makarov's fleet he feels exceedingly depressed, and asks himself what is about to happen! Eagerly he follows the course of the war, while reproaching himself for his anxiety which is unworthy of a Christian. "It must go from defeat to defeat and end by a dreadful overthrow." [1] The military operations are necessary, he admits, but they are gruesome. The thought of the starvation and poor equipment of the army gives him no peace. He feels that God has great plans for Russia, and he predicts that before long —possibly within a couple of years—religious freedom will follow as an outcome of this war, but he finds it hard to rejoice over it. The future seems so uncer-

[1] Quoted from the English original.

tain. "You feel that you are facing unheard of events. I know that the Japanese must win, but it hurts so."

On New Year's Day of 1905 he writes that he is looking forward to a "bad and formidable year." He has a close view of the dreadful nightmare of the so-called "January days," and he watches with interest but without much hope the political awakening and the dawn of freedom in Russia. He is naturally and entirely a man of peace, deeds of violence repelling him even when he realises their worth, and he has possibly looked too deep into the wounded soul of the Russian people to believe in a cure by such means. The prevalent unrest is, of course, a great hindrance to the work, but nevertheless it is carried on, and he writes in 1905 in a letter to Mr. Wilder: [1] "I hope that if we are now in the hollow of a wave, a rise will come too. The 46th Psalm will become very real to some of us shortly."

Two years after the Russian Revolution Paul Nicolay was stricken by a great personal sorrow which might easily have driven him away from the young people to whom he was devoting his life. His dearest friend in Russia was, as we know, Alexander Maximovsky, who had faithfully helped him in his Christian work, especially among students. He had opened his home for the meetings of the Movement, visited students in their homes and helped them in many ways. Maximovsky was also known for his kind-heartedness and justice, and in every way as an unusual Russian official. In 1907 he fell prey to the blind terrorism which the revolutionary youth of Russia had seized as

[1] Quoted from the English original.

their only weapon, and was murdered by a fanatical "kursistka" during a reception in his office.

Paul Nicolay was greatly affected by the blow; in the first hours of his grief he said that he felt as if a part of himself had been taken away, that with the loss of his friend half of his life had gone. But his zeal for the Student Movement was not lessened by this loss. Maximovsky had died as a Christian, and on his death-bed had implored pardon for his murderess; and Paul Nicolay avenged the death of his friend by taking up the increasing burden of his work for the Russian Student Movement with his unalterable faithfulness. The Revolution had at least led to an increased freedom of public meetings and freedom of speech, which opened up new possibilities for free Christian teaching. Students of different higher educational institutions might now be invited to attend public lectures, whose purpose was to counteract the strong anti-Christian propaganda of the University and arouse at least an interest in Christianity. Occasionally well-known foreigners would speak with Baron Nicolay as interpreter; he acquired great skill in the difficult task of translating into Russian words spoken in English, German, or French. But it was more usually he himself who had to go into the fire, and it always seemed like a baptism of fire to him who never entirely overcame the feeling of discomfort, almost dread, which accompanied the giving of a public address.

Besides the definitely spiritual phase of the work Baron Nicolay had many practical cares connected with the arranging of lectures. Almost every time there was to be an outside speaker he had to go from one authority to another, uncertain to the last minute whether the necessary permission would be granted— the Police Commissioner would refer him to the City Prefect, who sent him to the Minister of the Interior or the Clerical Consistory, and these again to the Holy Synod—but as a rule Baron Nicolay succeeded, through his perseverance, in obtaining the precious permit. And in the hall, secured for the occasion with almost equal difficulty, several hundred students might often gather in their eagerness to hear about the World's Student Christian Federation, or to find the answer to the question: "Why do we need a Divine Savior?" or "Can an educated, thinking man believe in the Divinity of Jesus Christ?"

It was in 1908 that Baron Nicolay began to be especially interested in the latter theme, of whose basic significance for religious work he was aware, and he devoted himself with loving interest to its elaboration. The first time he spoke on that subject he felt that the audience remained untouched, and it seemed as if his task had been a complete failure. But courageously he repeated the experiment, this time with a very different result. During the ensuing years there was no other theme on which he spoke so often or with such great success. One of his co-workers tells of how he would occasionally be asked to deliver the same address twice in the course of one week with "Soljanoj Gorodok's" large hall filled both times. Tickets had been distributed, but there were not enough to go around; students and kursistki crowded into all the corridors. With glowing interest and tense expression they lis-

tened, eagerly grasping every word that might solve the
vital question: "Who was Christ?"

"And Christ is presented to them as the Son of God
in His rightful glory, and the heart of the Russian
youth, hitherto tormented by doubts, celebrates a joyful fête; for many now know why they are alive and
they greet each other with the customary Easter greeting, 'Risen indeed.' At one of these meetings there
was a student who had decided to put an end to her
life. During the preceding days she had even searched
for a place where she could without difficulty throw
herself under a tramway car. She had happened into
this meeting, and now she realised that life had a meaning and that she must not take her own life. On our
way home she said that she felt as if she were holding a
burning light as on Maundy-Thursday, and only feared
lest the flame might be extinguished on the way home.
But the flame burned on and increased in brightness.
She had found Christ, and began before long to work
for His Kingdom."

Does not this simple account sufficiently illustrate the
vast influence which these public meetings on apologetic
subjects came to exert on the student youth of Russia?
They also became of a truth a message of *salvation*.
Now as previously it was not always Baron Nicolay's
arguments, however well substantiated they were, as
much as the genuine conviction of faith behind them
that convinced his audience. To hear this highly cultured man openly confessing Christ, to see that he could

do it without "deadening his reason," or renouncing his right to historical investigation—this in itself was something new and great to many young people who wanted to believe "if only it were possible." But the refractory also were gripped by the spirit which pervaded the meeting. At the close of almost every address some of the audience asked to join Bible groups, where they were brought into touch with the Savior through the Book itself. The Gospel of Mark was usually the first to be studied by newcomers. Baron Nicolay prepared and had published at the close of 1906 a little "hand-book" for instruction for this, the simplest and shortest of the Gospels. The guide book consisted mostly of questions and references to different texts, and sought to lead beginners to independent reading and thorough Bible study. Not all those who joined the Bible groups continued to attend them; many disappeared after a short time. But lasting assets were also gained.

Baron Nicolay himself was far from always conscious of the great progress of the work and of his own growing influence. Again and again during the years following the Revolution can be found utterances of his which reflect weariness and a sense of failure. If several students demonstratively left the hall during an address, if the membership decreased in some years, the feeling that all had been in vain might steal over him. It was not the cause that was hopeless, not God who had forsaken His servant, but the servant who had not been equal to his task. He writes to Dr. Mott of the first public addresses in a characteristic way.[1] "As

[1] Quoted from the English original.

I was the lecturer and am not gifted as a speaker, the first and third lectures were not successful. . . ."

"I am not suited for this work—not that it could not succeed, but I am not suited," he once writes in his diary. "But I must endure through the winter for Mott's sake. . . ." "Too old, too weak, too nervous, too far removed from the students"—thus he characterises himself, and on another occasion he feels that he is "neither spiritually nor intellectually on that level which is required in order to deliver public addresses." But he endured, not only for Dr. Mott's sake, but also for the work itself, for God's sake; and at times a brighter outlook on the work was granted him. He could not fail to notice the hush that occasionally fell over the audience during his address, like a breath of the Spirit of the Eternal. He must even have noticed how God opened up for him one door after another "in that land where it is impossible to undertake anything unless God go before." Therefore he never *despairs,* although the field of labour be immense and the obstacles many and unforeseen. In his own anxiety and struggling he merely sees a pledge that God will bless the work. "You must bleed to bless," remains one of his characteristic sayings. And as an antidote for his tendency to focus his attentions on his own inability he loves to quote a phrase, used by his friend Mr. Wilder: "God's biddings are God's enablings."

In 1907 Baron Nicolay, on his way to Japan to take part in a conference of the World's Student Christian Federation, started the work in Moscow, where a Movement was soon to be formed having the same basis as that at St. Petersburg. A Miss D. took charge of this

work, giving up her own interests in order to give herself unreservedly to the cause of the students. "She
fights for Christ like a lioness," was the verdict of Miss
Rouse, who visited Moscow as well as several other
Russian cities. In 1910 the Movement spread to Kieff.
The net was beginning to envelop many Russian University towns, in Dorpat and Riga the foundations for
the work having already been laid.

The difficult task of organising the work at all these
centres fell also to Baron Nicolay. Local leaders came
to him with all their troubles; and he it was who forged
together the links of the movement from the different
unions, and also formed and maintained connections
with the organisations of other lands. It was difficult
to find men suited to lead Bible study groups or take
charge of the practical side of the work; and as the
Movement spread Baron Nicolay was forced to look
for helpers from America. Many of these assistants
proved to be both suitable and interested, but the Russian language was a great stumbling-block to them. To
give them a true understanding of the Russian nature
—so unlike the American—and to reconcile the students' sensitive nationalism to these foreign leaders
was not always easy. The "American" question as
well as that of the unconfessional character of the
Movement were brought up for many a heated debate
at Association meetings, and caused a good deal of irri-
tation among the members. To strive to smooth over
these controversies without losing any of the accessible
working power became an added task for the leader of
the Movement.

Thus the grain of mustard seed had grown into a

large tree, and the quiet humble gardener had enough
to do in tending it. The manner of its growth can
most clearly be followed by quoting some excerpts
from Baron Nicolay's letters to Dr. Mott—modest,
positive accounts of his work. We begin with a letter
written in 1910 and referring, among other things, to
the matter of the Americans newly arrived.[1]

"You will have heard by this time that some unfortunate misunderstanding has taken place in choosing Mr.
A. for the Mayak,[2] and that Mr. G. finds that he cannot be of any help there. . . . The thought naturally
came to me that *'maybe'* this misunderstanding might
be part of God's plan to give *us* another helper besides
Mr. D., but that everything depended on Mr. A.'s personality. The issues at stake are so great that we cannot afford to take a man only to keep him from going
back to America, and that the wrong man in Russia
would be the worst disaster that could befall us. I
thought that the first requisite would be that the man
for Russia should have come to Jesus Christ himself
and have found in Him his personal Savior. Sec-
ondly, that he should be a teachable, prudent, thoughtful, prayerful and sympathetic man, willing to learn
before teaching others, and willing, first of all, to learn
to know the situation; thirdly—a man with Bible
knowledge and experience in Bible study work, and a
full-fledged student. I gave much weight to Mr. D.'s
impression of Mr. A., but wanted also to judge for myself. This evening we had a good bit of conversation

[1] Quoted from the original English letter.
[2] Russian branch of the Y.M.C.A.

and I found that on all these mentioned points he seems to answer the demands. . . .

"You will be glad to hear that the Moscow students are working with heroic devotedness and that their number is growing. I wish it was the same spirit here. Some of our members have even fallen off. I have held a series of addresses [three themes] with a satisfactory attendance, and as a result about two dozen men have entered Bible circles, but some of them will again fall off, very likely.

"I intend soon to go to Kieff to try to pick up the thread where I dropped it last autumn, but I really do not know if it is wise to give public student addresses and form circles without having anybody on the spot to carry it on.

"In Odessa some five to six men are trying to form a group and ask me to come, but there too it would hardly be advisable to launch out.

"And yet, on the other hand, when you hear of almost daily suicides of students and hear how they are groping in the dark, you feel most anxious to help at least some by evangelistic meetings.

"Mr. D. is doing nicely. The men like him and seem to feel him one of them. . . . He does not seem to be a linguist, but by dint of perseverance he will certainly master enough of the language to speak fluently next autumn, and make himself understood.

"Our monthly periodical, the 'Listok,' is being carried on with fairly good success. . . ."

A letter dated April 26, 1910, gives us a still more

vivid picture of Baron Nicolay as a pioneer and organiser:[1]

"Your and Mr. S.'s very kind lines reached me when
I was on the point of starting for Moscow, Kieff and
Odessa, so I preferred delaying my answer until I had
seen the latter places. In Moscow Miss D.'s and A.'s
zeal and faithful devotedness to their work is beyond
all praise. Ten women's groups and six or seven for
men are in existence. . . . A certain friction between
the pietistic and the intellectual element is being felt
there. . . . I hope they will pull together, understanding how necessary both currents are. I asked an
experienced man and woman student to come with us
to Kieff. Their assistance has proved to be exceptionally valuable, and I hope to be able to repeat the experiment in the future.

"In Kieff (13,000 students) the character of the
place and students is somewhat different from Moscow. The Jews are numerous and form a compact
group. The present attitude of the young educated
Jews and Jewesses is most interesting. They cling to
their nation on national grounds, but feel themselves
estranged from their orthodox co-religionaries intellectually and morally. They have perverted views about
Christianity (no wonder), have no ideals, no hopes,
and are as in a wood not knowing which way to turn.
Their mental keenness and openness are promising. The
Poles (Catholics) form another compact group, a world
for themselves; many rich dandies among them. An
interesting religious movement is making itself felt

[1] Quoted from the original English letter.

among the Catholic students too, and gives us points of contact with a few individuals. The Russian men and women students in Kieff seem inferior to the Moscovites in independence and energy. Official oppression is more keen and they live more solitary lives, especially the kursistki. This is said to be the cause of many suicides. On the other hand, the Moscovite kursistka who helped me in Kieff says there is more interest among the women students for religious questions in Kieff than in Moscow.

"I gave two lectures—one on the Diety of Christ with 500 attendants, men and women students only, and one on a religious theme: "What reality can Christ bring into our lives," with 200, and the behavior of the audience was good. Ninety took inquiry cards,[1] but only 12 sent them to me. The upshot of over a fortnight's stay was one woman's group of 10 and two men's groups of five or six reliable members in each—after the chaff had fallen off. God's assistance was especially visible in our finding leaders whom God seemed to have prepared. I find the result meagre, but suppose a first beginning must be small in this country.

"The new members are in full sympathy with our principles. One Catholic and one Jew are among them. I might say two Catholics, but one is a young French Abbot who has learned some Russian, has entered the University, and has, I suppose, plans of his own. . . .

"I came to Odessa only to reconnoitre the ground in view of my possibly returning here for a longer

---

[1] Cards on which those who wished to come into touch with the Student Movement might write their name and address.

stay in the autumn. I was astonished to find that a group of six or seven was already in existence. All but one are pious young Baptist youths, as yet green and narrow, but capable of widening, I hope, and very willing. The exceptional one is an interesting fellow of Bulgarian extraction, an old student, formerly an atheist and in touch with the radicals, who has gradually been brought to a real conversion to God and has united with the Baptists. Unfortunately, he is graduating this spring and is not certain where he will be next autumn. If possible he would like to be a teacher in this town, but his religion may be an obstacle.

"If the next conference [1] is to be in Constantinople, would that not bring you over to Europe earlier and give us a chance of seeing you in Kieff, Kharkoff, and Odessa? . . . If you come it will need preparing the ground and forming local associations before you arrive to preserve the results, and lots of prayer to open the way for you and counteract the opposition of the influential clerical spheres. All things are possible with God."

Jews, Poles, Russians, Bulgarians—what a motley crowd this letter brings before us! In many places the work included Germans, Esthonians, Latvians, and even Armenians and Caucasians. It required an eye alert to the needs of all, familiarity with the character of the different nationalities so as to avoid driving students away from the Movement by underrating anything which might be essential to their particular

[1] That of the World's Student Christian Federation.

national tendencies or church traditions. Baron Nicolay attacked the work with an indefatigable will to understand, "himself to learn, before teaching others," and with an untiring search for the essentials concealed behind external religious forms. The centre of Christianity was for him "not a creed, but a personality"—the person of Jesus, a living Power with whom the souls of men might be brought into touch. *"Christians are people in whom to a larger or smaller, degree dwells the Spirit of Christ,"* was the broad-minded definition of Christianity which he once gave. The way was not so important. But while Nicolay was willing, in compliance with the bases of the World's Student Christian Federation, to admit members of all Christian churches and sects into the Movement, he never permitted any one church or sect to usurp power within it. This position naturally caused dissatisfaction among reactionary Russian circles, and at times within the movements themselves there did arise a strong opposition to its non-sectarianism.

The *external* resistance was usually formulated in refusals to allow Christian student leaders to speak because of criticism coming from ecclesiastical sources. Thus we read in a letter dated November 27, 1910, from Kharkoff to one of the secretaries of the Student Christian Movement in Finland:

"The 'peculiar' director of police in Odessa refused to let me hold a meeting there without gaining permission from the Bishop, who was not disposed to grant it as he did not know me and had only read unfavourable accounts of me. I left the town and hur-

ried to the unsightly town of Nikolajev, from which
I arrived here a week ago. It is rather trying to meet
obstacles of that kind, but I now believe that it was
for the best, and I can now see 'in what ways the
Lord performs His work' as you expressed it. That
promise has literally been fulfilled. The Lord has
prepared the way, opened doors, and removed obstacles, and I have been able to see how He went ahead
of me performing His work."

The "peculiar" director of police in Odessa was
none other than the notorious General Tolmatscheff,
whose hostile attitude towards Baron Nicolay was not
only characteristic of himself but also of a whole
class of Russian officials in the time of the Czar. He
explained the refusal by stating that there was a German colony near the city, "therefore the situation is
serious." When Baron Nicolay ventured to remark
that his addresses had not been considered dangerous
in other places where he had obtained permission to
speak, the pompous reply was: "What occurs in other
places does not affect me. But my principle is always
to go hand in hand with the clergy."

If Baron Nicolay felt it "rather trying to meet obstacles of that kind," he soon had to learn to submit
to far more insulting refusals. In 1911 the authorities at Moscow rejected a plea for permission for Miss
Rouse to address the women students by reason of
certain paragraphs in the speech, branding the whole
address, as "a danger to public morality and a men-
ace to public peace." The address was on "The Social, Moral and Religious Problems of Students." The

Bishop of Kieff was more frank in explaining that the addresses were not wanted, as the efforts of a foreigner to win students to the cause of religion might lead them to an unfortunate comparison with the priesthood who had done nothing for them. Several years later an influential authority of the church said that his only objection to the Student Christian Movement was that it was led by Baron Nicolay, *who was a Baptist*. In many cases the hostility of the clergy was based on the idea that Nicolay was a sectarian apostate from the Orthodox Church, but when it was made clear that he had been a Lutheran from the very first his work was usually regarded with milder eyes.

But the misunderstandings were not always cleared up. The annoyances of the authorities were often caused by attacks in the press, many of them founded on complete lies. The ecclesiastical papers published the most incredible tales about the groups of Christian students. They insisted that the men students met for Bible study with their hats on and cigarettes in their mouths, and that the leaders were illiterate, low-minded men. From an entirely different source—radicalism— dangerous darts were occasionally hurled at the Movement, as when one newspaper declared that the "well-known conservative," Baron Nicolay, was arranging religious meetings for the purpose of drawing students away from politics—a serious accusation in the eyes of the student world—and added that the students "remain more than indifferent to these attempts!"

Here it was indeed necessary to utilise "the weapons of salvation on the right hand and on the left," and the life of the Russian Student Movement acquired its own individual character from the militant stand it was forced to take against its will. Letters to the Finnish Secretary give us a glimpse into the constant warfare of the groups and their leaders against obstacles and dangers within and without. The hardest battle centred around the statutes of the Movement in St. Petersburg, which were presented in 1912 to the Minister of the Interior in the hope of securing for the Movement a legally secure existence. In January of 1912 Baron Nicolay writes:

"The work is most seriously menaced in Moscow where the clergy are more powerful than elsewhere. We wanted to distribute among the students 10,000 brief printed notices of Sherwood Eddy's coming visit, but the police would not permit it. It is so irksome to be continually uncertain and have to bicker with that kind of authority. At times comes the thought that we must not worry, for the Lord will surely lead the work on to victory even as He led the Israelites out of Egypt with a strong and mighty arm, although the outlook seemed so hopeless. But I am very, very grateful for the prayers of my friends which sustain me."

A month later he writes:

"The outlook on our work here is quite menacing and the work may be forbidden at any time, for the Ministry of the Interior now follows absolutely in the tracks of the Holy Synod. All is well in Kieff, and we are getting as many new members as we can admit, about 25 men and probably the same number of women. We have now made a beginning here.[1] We had hoped we might be permitted to speak once at the Polytechnical Institute which has 6,000 students. But no answer has come from Moscow. Our request has been forwarded to the Missionaries ["the inquisitors"],[2] who are almost certain to give a negative reply. The situation in the group at Moscow is so pitiful that I am especially praying for leaders. Help with your intercession."

Later in the spring he finds more favourable news to impart from Moscow, and continues:

"We have good news from Kieff, God be praised. Mr. Eddy writes that about sixty are seriously taking part in Bible groups. Can you imagine it, I have received 890 roubles for our work from an unknown person! It is as if the sky were beginning to brighten. The Minister of the Interior has informed one of my friends that he has no intention of hindering our work. That is all we need. Perhaps God will now lead us out of our distress and let us continue unhindered. This has been brought about by the prayers of our friends. Maybe we may still hope to see our statutes confirmed. Maybe it will even be possible to speak in other cities without getting permission from the clergy. What we now most need is men who can give their whole time as secretaries. Mr. Eddy has promised to procure part of the necessary finance, but who is suited for the position? I have written S., but as he has now such a bright future ahead can it be expected, or even hoped,

1 In St. Petersburg.
2 The so-called Missionaries in Russia were often commissioned to keep an eye on sects and were notorious for their methods.

that he should give it all up in order to devote himself to our work? Help us also in this need."

On these two important matters, the need of leaders and the statutes presented to the Minister of the Interior, Baron Nicolay writes to Dr. Mott in June of the same year: [1]

"Of course the real crucial question is in getting Russian leaders, like Miss K. in Kieff; men or women who have grown out of our Movement—godly, devoted, energetic, and wise workers. They must be God-given, and I daily pray for them. We have two more in view. . . . One is overscrupulous and the other has not yet given his definite answer. Both men would be excellent. . . . We have received pressing invitations from Kazan, and a group promises to form itself there in the autumn. Another ripe field is Dorpat, where some still remember you and are very friendly. Everywhere the ground is prepared by God, and as our main lines and principles are now proved by experience and put into form in print, they are more readily understood in new places.

"But as the critical moment of confirming or refusing our statutes by the government draws nigh the opposition and attacks of part of the clergy become more violent. A very prominent professor in Kieff has printed a dastardly, mean, lengthy article against us in a leading clerical paper, poisoning the minds against us in wide circles. This drew forth a refutation by Professor S. (of Kieff), but the clerical paper would not accept it, and we had to print it in a secular paper.

[1] Quoted from the original English letter.

Fancy our opponent ending by saying: 'If you wish to destroy the State and the Church, then for that end the Student Christian Movement will be eminently useful.' Professor S.'s lengthy answer is good. I did not know that his interest in us had gone far enough for him to be willing to commit himself in this way, but since he has now done it he has proved to be the faithful friend of the Movement. Mme. O. has rendered us invaluable help. You will find her a very superior woman in every respect. She is trusted and respected in all official and court circles and has access everywhere. She asked for an interview with the Minister of Interior, and had a very satisfactory conversation with him. She called on some other ministers, and very ably defended our cause. The remark of one of the officials, who refused our statutes last autumn and who was much more frank with her than with me, was quite characteristic. 'If Dr. Mott presents the petition it will certainly be refused. If Baron Nicolay presents it, it will very likely be refused because he is a Protestant. But if you present it, it will very likely be confirmed.' . . ." She told the Overprocurator of the Holy Synod: 'You know how attached I am to my church; but if I had to choose between my church and the Student Movement I would choose the latter.' She impressed one of our worst enemies, an arch-bishop of great influence. And so we handed in our petition, with a memorandum to the Minister of Interior signed by her. We got another short memorandum, recommending the usefulness of an Association like ours, signed by a priest and three professors, of whom two are prominent men in the eyes of the government; and now the die is cast, and during the summer we will either at last have official permit or definite refusal. I need not say how much is at stake; you understand it yourself and will certainly remember us in prayer. Now that three professors in St. Petersburg have committed themselves for us, we have good hope of drawing them into closer contact with us. After our autumn leaders' conference to which Professor S. of Kieff has promised to come, we intend to make use of his presence for a series of open meetings for students and begin the term with a strong campaign. If we have but one good professor with us, the others will follow.

"You will have heard that we have given up the idea of putting Mr. D. into independent work in Dorpat. After a conversation I had with a trusted student of ours who went there with him for a reconnoitring tour, I saw I had been too hasty in proposing this step. Mr. D. may be ready for it in a year or two, but not yet. So this next winter he intends to concentrate his efforts on work specially among University students in St. Petersburg, together with N. who promises to be a delightful companion. We are sorry we have no other man to send over with him now to America, but the language is such a draw-back. He is a truly devoted Christian, a soft, somewhat emotional character, no leader, but an excellent helper and worker.

"You will have heard of Mr. A's. plans for Lesnoi of renting the other half of the upper floor for a foyer. I think it the very thing to do, and much better than launching out on a hostel on a large scale.

"We are hoping at our autumn leaders' conference to form a National Union, and have sent the proposed statutes to Moscow and Kieff. If we succeed, and if we work well this coming winter, it may be possible we will be accepted into the Federation together— maybe—with Bulgaria and Servia?"

This letter is that of a leader, one might almost say of a commander. One can see him studying his battle field, all the larger University centres of Russia, placing the right man in the right place, gathering countless threads into his hand. And how easily one might forget the sleepless nights of the commander, the inner loneliness and crushing responsibilities of the leader, often threatening to become too much for him who sent the quiet, clear reports to America. We learn of almost daily neuralgic headaches, of a burning longing for fellowship with mature Christians of his own age, of the old "death anguish" before each public address—and we understand the oft repeated plea for the intercession of his friends, for the strength which is made perfect in weakness. The task was growing and the opportunities multiplying; yet the fight was still far from over. In a letter to Helsingfors dated from Monrepos, October 11, 1912, we read of victories won and of new hopes.

". . . Thursday the 8th I had to speak, and I had seldom found it so hard nor felt as despondent and depressed. But as I began to speak I was carried through safely, borne by the arms of prayer, and all went well, thanks to God. To-morrow is an important day. Our case (our statutes) is then to be decided upon by the Minister of the Interior. Just think, here at the conference they came to a unanimous resolution to form a Student Christian Movement for the whole of Russia! It is a great joy to me. In a few hours I am leaving for St. Petersburg with a deep sense of gratitude to God. I have seen that the field which the Lord in His mercy has called on me to plant has begun to sprout, that other workers are willing to devote their lives to it, and that the Lord has permitted the conference to end with rich blessing. I have seen more clearly than ever before that it is far better to lose one's life for others than to find one's life. The egotistical life tries so often to dominate me again and draw me away from a life of service. But may God grant me strength never to cease to seek His Kingdom first."

Soon it became evident that the matter of the statutes would not be solved as quickly as had been hoped. The Holy Synod at a meeting presided over by the Metropolitan of Moscow, an enemy of the Student Movement, drew up an official resolution against the recognition of the Movement—"One way of binding the hands of the Ministry of the Interior," as Paul Nicolay put it. Fresh attacks by the clerical press followed. Their one solace was that Mme. O. later succeeded in persuading the Minister of the Interior to promise that no obstacles should be laid in the way of the work, for it had even been urged, at the meeting of the Holy Synod, that the group be broken up and the matter called to the attention of the Czar. In March of 1913 Baron Nicolay writes to Dr. Mott that the Statutes are permanently buried in the Ministry of the Interior. And in this their grave they remained at rest until December, 1917, when their ratification was followed by the beautiful but short-lived promise of free and legally sanctioned activity.

But through all these conditions the work was carried on. In a letter to Dr. Mott dated October, 1913, Baron Nicolay rejoices over a successful conference of leaders. A spirit of peace and harmony had prevailed, practical matters had been discussed to advantage—which had not always been the case—and the delegates who had been in America showed that they had been benefited by what they had learned there. Baron Nicolay had also only words of praise for his young Russian assistants, N., and especially M., who for the sake of the work had given up his good position in the State school and torn himself away from a town where he was universally loved and respected, "a good speaker and a Nathanael in whom there is no guile, a truly converted soul." It is of great significance that this man remained a member of the Greek Orthodox Church.

The professors now began to give more active assistance. The entire year immediately preceding the World War becomes a time of revivals among Russian students. It is true that in Dorpat and Riga there was a falling away, but in the purely Russian cities, especially Moscow and Kieff, the situation is very different. In Kieff the number of Bible groups has increased, and in Moscow the numbers crowding

to the Sunday meetings in the two medium sized rooms
of the Movement increase to 270, and as the rooms
are almost entirely lacking in ventilation the atmosphere becomes so unbearably close that "if not at least
four or five are carried out in a faint the programme
is not considered complete." It is about a meeting
in Moscow—this time in a large hall as there were
five hundred present—that Baron Nicolay writes to
the Finnish Secretary: "There was something in the
air that bore me up, made the audience attentive, and
led 60 men and 75 women students to give their addresses, showing their desire to be invited to our meetings. I can only explain this as an outcome of the
Day of Prayer, when thousands of prayers throughout the world, including yours and those of the dear
friends in Helsingfors, interceded for poor, dark Russia. Mott was right when he suggested making use
of the days of prayer and the ensuing days for active
meetings. In St. Petersburg also a large number gathered on the Day of Prayer for Students to hear M.'s
address, and the results were good."

Thousands of prayers went up from the student
world for "poor, dark Russia," helping hands were
stretched forth from many a place to her youth in
their struggle for a religious and moral awakening,
and the Russian Student Christian Movement began
in spite of the "non possumus" of the government to
be felt as a factor in the common conscience of the
student world. When the war broke out this was the
situation, and the result of the work which Paul Nicolay in fear and trembling had undertaken fifteen years
before.

We have been following the rapid development and growth of the Student Christian Movement under the leadership of Paul Nicolay. But so far only the external contours of the Movement have been shown, only the attempts at organisation, the struggle for existence and the mastery over new fields of labour presented. Is the inner worth of this work comparable to the relatively large external apparatus? Was the cause itself worthy of the pain it cost? This question involuntarily arises in the mind of him who has followed along in the battle. Let us therefore recall the purpose for which the Movement was founded, what its leaders and patrons hoped to accomplish through it. Their work was to wage war against the worst enemies of the Russian student—loneliness and moral uncertainty. They wanted to transform as many as possible of them into strong and happy people, able and willing to serve their oppressed and suffering countrymen in a positive and creative way. They desired above all, in spite of the theories and suppositions of the time, to bring them to the one and only reality, the finding of their soul. Had the goal been reached? Miss Marie Bréchet replied to this question at Paul Nicolay's grave with the following words:

"Through him hundreds of despairing, lost and seeking souls have discovered the way to a living faith in God. They have been changed into *happy people* who have found their ideal and the power to lead a better life. Baron Nicolay has ushered in a new epoch into the religious life of Russia. Through the Movement Russia has obtained Christian teachers, able to give to the youth answers to "the forbidden questions," physicians, not powerless in face of soul suffering, educated workers in various fields, who have learned loyally and honestly to perform their duty."

In the discussion of the external growth of the Movement we have now and then caught a glimpse of some young person standing on the verge of destruction when the saving message reached him. But to bring a message was not the only task of the Student Movement; it aimed to offer the youth a steadying influence, the warmth of a home, opportunities for development. It aimed to educate them through what some one has called the "sacrament of fellowship." All this became part of the daily task of the Movement, at the centre of whose life—most especially in St. Petersburg—stood that man who had said, even in the early years of the Movement, that he was "too old, too weak, too far removed from the students"—Pavel Nikolajevitsch, the mere mention of whose name would light up the face of a member of the Movement.

By listening to the conversation of St. Petersburg students about their Christian Movement—"krusjok" (the circle) as they call it, one is impressed by its being to them much more than is usually true of a Movement—a home, a bright spot in their existence. "Do you remember the party we had one spring, the flowers, the singing? How hard it was to leave, for there was *resurrection* in the air." They have so many mutual reminiscences—Bible Study in the tiny rooms of the student members, summer conferences, picnics, and even the work itself with the exciting campaigns during the autumn in the institutions to which they belonged, and at the close of semesters the planning for work in the home towns to which they were returning. They know that they have "krusjok" to thank for much of what they are—perhaps for all. And in the course of the conversation you are sure to hear, "And do you remember Pavel Nikolajevitsch— that time, and that?"

The students recall how he usually began the meetings, with his quiet and friendly greeting to one and another as they arrived, inquiring about their health and their work, and encouraging the discouraged by a loving and understanding word, or with a joke containing a serious meaning. "Ye, Pharaoh's lean cattle," he says to those who only "swallow" talks and addresses and emotions, but never grow nor are willing to share with others. And the students laugh genially. They do not take offence, not even when the reprimand comes in a sharper form, as it occasionally does. If he were absent from a meeting it seemed empty without him, even if he had not been scheduled to speak. And how great was not his worth in discussions on the practical side of organization, when they became too excited or irritated and when in their eagerness, in a truly Russian way, they wandered from the point. His gentle but clear voice would then be raised to call them back to the main and the really important theme, and even the temperate, almost monotonous tones, had a beneficial effect on such occasions. But when he rose to give a devotional address his words, in spite of their completely unadorned simplicity, often penetrated deeper than those of others, not setting the emotions into vibration but stimulating the conscience and arousing the will.

And every one remembers Baron Nicolay at the Conferences—that autumn evening, for instance, when about ninety students got off the train at Wiborg Station, and the first thing they saw on the platform was Pavel Nikolajevitsch's familiar face, and the grey cap waved in welcome. It was he who saw them all on the local train for the station near Monrepos, he who had provided that on their arrival they should be supplied with lanterns, and he who led the gay procession to the villas where they were to stay. His love and his thoughtfulness were revealed in every detail and in all the arrangements. And the days of the Conference were beneficial, not only spiritually, but they were also wonderful days of rest, when overworked students grown pallid with the unhealthy life of the big city might wander about in the woods, inhaling with pleasure the fresh scent of the pines, later to do credit with large appetites to the bountiful meals—flowing with milk if not with honey—where they might really eat until they were satisfied. On the walks Baron Nicolay would arm himself with fir cones which he later, with true aim, showered upon his young guests, who were not slow to retaliate. One of the days of the conference was christened "Sergej" day, when the three delegates, Sergej by name, were awakened in the morning by Pavel Nikolajevitsch presenting each with a carnation stuck into a fir cone with a comically ceremonious speech. They would never again see a fir cone or a carnation without recalling the happy incident.

But it was not only at meetings and conferences that Baron Nicolay met students. During the long semesters in St. Petersburg he lived with them in their daily life, sharing in their sorrows and hardships. They came to him in times of temptation and doubt, and he would listen to their confused youthful effusions by the hour, never begrudging them a time of much needed rest. These interviews were often a real trial to him who liked clear cut lines in everything and was by no means impulsive, but he never avoided them, knowing that in this respect also he was called to bear the burdens of others. Then he would often go to see students in their rooms, never letting long distances or steep steps hinder him in this. He tells of how he once suddenly had the inspiration to call on a certain student, and how he found him in a shattered condition, and persuaded him to consecrate himself wholly to God. And this case is certainly only one of many similar ones.

Baron Nicolay kept pace with the development of the members of the group, sought to hinder their throwing themselves into the life of the Movement with an enthusiasm which might cause their studies to suffer, or from isolating themselves too much in their studies—two extremes which were always having to be balanced. He sought to instil in them respect for quiet, regular work and the significance of self-discipline. Characteristic of the way he thus acquired of treating overexcited young people is the story of a student who came to him with the information that he would have to leave the Movement as he had lost his faith. Baron Nicolay looked at him and realised that what he had lost was not his faith, but "faith in his faith." So he

entirely ignored the statement, and simply asked the
amazed young man to mail some parcels of Movement
literature and do a couple of other errands. The youth
departed; and never again did he repeat his intention
of leaving the Movement. Baron Nicolay was very
unlike the lively, emotional southerners, but that in itself helped make intercourse with him helpful to them,
and his words and whole nature acted on them like a
cool, refreshing douche. Yet no one could doubt that
fundamentally he felt more keenly than most of them
for the individual members and for the common cause.

Not in the spiritual alone, but also in purely practical
matters did Baron Nicolay become a stay to his students. It was he who superintended the furnishing
of the room for meetings—the Movement having for
a long time been housed in his own rooms—and in so
doing he attended to the smallest details. Former members of the Movement tell how he ordered for the
room in the new building a sofa, which was to be broad
enough that in case of need—and such was often the
case—two students might be able to spend the night on
it. Men came to him with all their troubles. One day
a student who was ill was brought to the Movement
headquarters by his friends who did not feel like leaving him alone in his miserably cold room. He was
very ill, and it was Paul Nicolay who now took him in
charge. It was he who sent for a doctor, called an
automobile, and brought him straight to the hospital.

Another student, a Christian medical, who had been
active in the work of the Movement, was for a long
time ill in a hospital in St. Petersburg. He came from
the South and could not stand the cold climate, but was

attacked by an ailment which finally developed into rapid consumption. As he now lay in the hospital, far from his own people, it was "Pavel Nikolajevitsch," the cheery and comforting friend, who came to see him every day. "His illness is a great grief to me," wrote Nicolay in a letter to Finland, and he did not exaggerate. "After his death we saw Pavel Nikolajevitsch one day, sad and dejected, accompanying his young friend in bitterly cold weather and on foot to his eternal resting place in a distant cemetery," writes Miss Marie Bréchet. And again we must remember that the young Caucasian was by no means the only one who in the hour of pain and death itself had this faithful, fatherly comforter by his side.

But there was especially *one* way of helping the young people he loved which seemed most effective to Baron Nicolay, and which he never neglected. He had learned to appreciate what an English Christian once said, that when it is useless to talk *to* a person it may be a great help to talk *about* him to God. He prayed a great deal for his students, and often urged his friends to pray for them. Letters already quoted have shown how frequently he asked for intercession for the whole Movement, but there are also often requests for individual members in his letters. In September, 1910, he writes as follows to the Secretary of the Finnish Movement in Helsingfors:

"One of our most promising young men writes that he must resign from the Movement as he is not fit for it. Evidently his feet must have slipped during the summer. I am praying God to bring him back. An eager young student came and promised to join a Bible group. He has been completely confused by all kinds of philosophy, and is also worried about his health, as he thinks he is threatened with consumption. If only the Spirit of God might take possession of him so that our friendship may not be reduced, as often happens, to nothing of spiritual value. Pray for him."

Another time he writes: "Poor S.[1] I have not yet seen him, but have learned that he has turned away from God and us, and we must now seek him by a detour, by way of heaven. Help us with him."

And later he writes: "Poor Z. has joined a Bible group, but one which is so far from the centre of the city, about an hour's journey, and a group which is weak and without a proper leader. Let us remember that prayer is not only one important way of furthering God's Kingdom, but the most important. If only unhappy Z. might get what he is looking for. About S., I heard that he came to see me to-day, and that he longs for Christian fellowship again as he finds his life so empty. God be praised. This should encourage us to continue in prayer."

There was one group among the students whom Baron Nicolay felt to be in greater need of spiritual help than others—those who were or might become leaders. He often bemoaned the lack of personalities for leadership in Russia. Once he wrote as follows: "The young people themselves are so devoid of energy and practical sense that they resemble freight cars without an engine." Orators, eager workers, and even

[1] The young seeker before mentioned.

geniuses could be found, but very few with the talent
for organisation and the ability both to command and
subordinate themselves—a requisite for a man or
woman in a position of responsibility.   A Dane has
told how, during a visit to the group at Moscow, he
became attached to a fine young man with an animated
and intelligent expression and a most attractive appearance. He told Baron Nicolay that he thought he would
in time become a leader in the Movement. "Hardly,"
was the brief reply; "he is a genius, and I do not believe in geniuses."   These words no doubt reflected a
bitter experience.   Leaders, true leaders, could not be
selected by human calculation, they must be given from
above, and that was why he prayed, as his letters show,
both *about* and *for* them.

The members of the Movement often realised that
they caused Baron Nicolay concern.   Sometimes they
did not rightly construe his purposes, and occasionally,
in spite of his tact and desire to be just, he might judge
them too severely, or his ways might repel some young
person of a distinctly æsthetic or philosophical tendency or unusually sensitive nature. But as a rule students were impressed by the steadfast good-will concealed behind the severity, and willingly took the blame
for all misunderstandings.   One of them said that
what amazed him most was Pavel Nikolajevitsch's per-
petual patience.   He marvelled in many a meeting
at his not "simply losing his temper with the students
and leaving the meeting."

But Paul Nicolay never left the meetings, neither
did he abandon the Movement because of occasional
jars. For he never went *his* way, but the Master's.

He became to the Russian students an example of loyalty and perseverance. Long after their student days were over and they had gone out into the world—scattered to countless country districts or plunged into the human sea of the larger cities—they retained their impression of him and thought of him as a "ray of light which had fallen across their path." Many came back to him for advice and help even in later years, and were always welcomed with joy and warmth. And he followed them when far away with his strong and ceaseless intercession.

When the great, and at first incredible and incomprehensible, reality of the World War broke into the life of the Russian Student Movement, it was impossible to tell whether it was to be favourable or harmful to the Movement. But it was evident to all that it would have to undergo a great change. One obstacle to the work would certainly be the rising spirit of nationalism.

On September 28, 1914, Baron Nicolay wrote Dr. Mott from St. Petersburg:[1] "Our work suffers greatly from this dreadful war. We can hold no public meetings and are reduced to members' meetings in a quiet way, for prayer and devotional purposes. In Kieff, Moscow, and here the women are sewing for the wounded and we are trying to do something in the way of visiting the wounded, giving Scripture portions and helping as we may.

"This war is like a constant nightmare, but God is thereby shaking the nations as never before since

[1] Quoted from the original English letter.

the days of Napoleon, and will no doubt make it serve
His cause. But what about Missions? Should the
days of mission work be ended and this be the beginning of God's judgments issuing in Christ's return?
The social upheavals after this war will be worse
than the war itself, I fancy.

"What would you advise our members to do as
long as this war lasts? Prayer-meetings? Devotional
meetings? Your advice would be important. . . .

"How I pine to see men of intelligence and spirit and
energy guide this poor Movement. I feel myself getting old and am asking God to raise up the right men,
especially (1) a good secretary for St. Petersburg and
(2) a good General Secretary. God grant that Sw.
and maybe Sc. may return after the war to this country. Russians are so flabby—sometimes it's enough
to make you despair.

"Fancy the B. & F. Bible Society here with no
funds for the distribution of Scriptures and the soldiers
so eager to have some. We'll do what we can, but it
won't suffice."

November 17th he wrote a few lines about the
Union in St. Petersburg which was going down hill
while those in Moscow and Kieff were doing well, and
added: [1]

"This is just the weak point with the men. When
I was always living in St. Petersburg and could devote
all my time and thought to the work here, a nucleus
grew around me. When I began to visit other towns,
I always found that during a six weeks' absence the
work had gone down.

[1] Quoted from the original English letter to Dr. Mott.

"I am sad to think that all these years of work have brought about so little results, that we have not even reached the fringe of the student world of Russia, and that if I were to fail now before we are legalised the work may crumble to pieces in some parts at least. As long as the present wind blows we cannot hope to be officially recognised, and, therefore, no bequests to the work can be made which would safeguard its future financially, and no binding order can be introduced for our organisation.

"I am also sorry to think that if *I* were more efficient, had more strength, more energy, and organising capacity, things would be better off than they are; and I can't understand why God does not give us a real national secretary. I am getting old and am sometimes getting weary and pine for a younger head to take the work in tow.

"I would be only too glad for a man like Sw., but if the Russians object to having a foreign leader, what is to be done?

"I know you have enough weights of your own to bear, and if I mention this it is only that you should know the inside. If we were to be organised and legalised like the Mayak, it would mean for us to sell our religious freedom and our high principles of internationalism and interdenominationalism."

A year later Baron Nicolay has a good report to give of the work in Moscow where he has just been. "The room where the meetings are held has been improved, electric light and electrical ventilators have been installed, so that cases of fainting from lack of air have become a thing of the 'happy past.' M. is holding meetings in the largest hall of the city, announcements on a large scale being possible and the crowds and police on friendly terms. Both men and women have shown more independence than in St. Petersburg. When the missionaries (spies) come they are permitted to remain through the meeting so as to be convinced in their own minds that nothing dangerous is being perpetrated. Recently a comical occurrence took place. A priest, who had never been to these meetings before, came to Miss S. and good-naturedly told her that he had been sent by a spy who could not decide whether or no the students were sectarians."

In St. Petersburg the work among the kursistki went well, and they flooded the hall for the joint meetings "like a wave." Those taking advanced courses had also formed a separate little Union working on their own initiative. The clergy began to be more sympathetic with the work.[1] "The meetings of a group at Priest J.'s continue once a week, and no harm is being done. Some find these meetings rather watery— some like them. Other priests are beginning to show some interest." The men students were the hardest to reach; not only the "weak and religious," but also the stronger ones. Baron Nicolay expresses his belief that they can not be reached through the printed page, but only through teaching of the right kind. "Otherwise they can be interested, but won't be impressed."

In the same letter we read: "You will be happy to hear that enterprising Miss T., finding the work closed in Kieff, is on the point of making a raid on Kazan

[1] Quoted from the original English letter.

and Saratoff. In the former town we have a former member of ours who is willing to conduct Bible classes, and in the latter town a number of Kieff students (and members, too) have settled and invited Miss K. to come. The University of Kieff has, you know, been evacuated to Saratoff.

"Every day we are expecting the orders calling the students for military service, beginning by the youngest classes. This will, of course, sadly cripple our work and oblige us to keep more in touch with our comrades at the front. Possibly the young students will first have to pass through some months of training to be made officers."

It is evident from this quotation that the war itself became a cause for the Student Christian Movement's penetrating deeper than ever before into the heart of Russia. Later it also became clear that the seeds which were carried by the storm winds to the Eastern parts of the country fell on good ground and bore fruit, in a time in which it seemed as if the whole planting was doomed to be uprooted. It is interesting to see how in a letter to one of his English friends in December, 1916, Baron Nicolay writes of this war, which became more and more of a hidden power whose activities it was impossible to follow. The letter also reveals much of the depth of the inner life of the writer at this critical time:[1]

"My dear friend, Mr. Sloan: It was a real joy to receive your very kind lines a couple of days ago, and I felt quite touched at your remembering me as you

[1] Quoted from the original English letter.

do. In the way of Christian fellowship with older Christians I have been cut off from this blessing for a long while, and so it warms my heart to remember the days spent with you in days gone by. What a joy it would be to meet you once again on this earth after all we are living through.

"I feel that with all the darkness around us, and maybe before us, we are to push on, doing our duty as we see it without looking far ahead or getting anxious, certain as it is to the eye of faith that God is working out His plans 'deep in unfathomable mines of never-failing skill.' God's Kingdom must gain by all that is going on. Great changes will take place which will open up new possibilities for the Kingdom of God, and one already now sees in contrast to a flood of wickedness of every kind overflowing its banks, a deepening of hunger for spiritual things in other circles.

"Many students are called for military service, and few are left. But among the women students the interest and the work are spreading as never before, into new places too. And there is much less arguing about Christianity and much more desire for positive truth than hitherto. In this I am much encouraged. Many students will in the ordeal of war become deepened and prepared for the Gospel's message. Years spent in captivity must, if not spoil, then reform many a man."

Like many others Baron Nicolay had, during the third year of the war, the feeling that since the night was so dark the dawn must be near. The following year brought great events and changes—but, instead of the expected peace, a revolution followed by new horrors. This revolution was greeted by Baron Nicolay with as little enthusiasm as that of the year 1905. He was, as we know, no friend of violent eruptions and could plainly see the evil forces in this movement. But the development of the student work was not hindered; on the contrary, in many ways it seemed that new opportunities were being opened up for it. On May 4, 1917, Baron Nicolay wrote to an English friend:[1]

". . . I feel really sincerely grateful to those who have been remembering me in prayer, and wish—thanking them most heartily—to say we have hitherto lacked nothing, and all has developed infinitely better than might have been expected. The whole situation in this country is a very delicate one, but He 'who saved' and 'still saves' will, we trust, still save and help. This thought has been a help to me, that if Christ orders us not to be anxious, it can only be on the ground that He means to take care. If He does not we must, if we may not He must. Either He or we.

"Immense changes have taken place. Can you fancy Russia with complete liberty of conscience, and holding meetings? Our students have on certain days been going through the streets selling New Testaments, and giving away 8,000 short Christian pamphlets which were most eagerly accepted. . . . At present the inner situation is very delicate and we can't foresee how it will unroll, but God will surely provide. All will be for the best of His Kingdom."

At this time, in spite of the many obstacles, the out-

[1] Quoted from the original English letter.

look seemed hopeful. The Movement in Petrograd was reaching new institutions, the students in Moscow were succeeding in raising money. In a letter to Dr. Mott written in December we read of the things Baron Nicolay has to rejoice over: [1] "One is that on December third the statutes of our Petrograd Association have at last been confirmed, and we are a legally recognised organisation after eight or nine years' struggling and waiting. Those of Moscow have not yet been confirmed on account of narrow formalism on the part of the local court. We will, however, gain the point in no distant future, and then we will be entitled to form a recognised federation for Russia.

"We are at a very low ebb at present, most of the students being in the army, and of the remaining very few caring to remain in university towns on account of the price of living and other reasons. When the army will be disbanded the students will be among the first to be let off, but at present studying is impossible.

"One bright spot on the dark picture is the development of a new centre in Odessa. In some places meetings have been held in schools, a thing impossible before. Our literature is being eagerly bought.

"I hope we will get your call for the Day of Prayer in good time. Prayer will be like a breath of ozone in a stifling atmosphere."

The atmosphere in Russia was indeed stifling. So little was known about the morrow, work was done as if at random, and only "with trembling" dared one rejoice over new victories won by the Movement. Gradually the prospects grew less bright while the ob-

[1] Quoted from the original English letter.

stacles began to loom larger. But even in the beginning of 1918 did Baron Nicolay keep his gaze fixed ahead in confidence that the work to which he had been called should not be destroyed.

"Our work has not been extinguished in Russia," he writes in February to Dr. Mott. . . . "It is too soon to decide anything about your coming to Russia next autumn. As yet travelling is next to impossible, and the students are scattered. Yet I trust God will bring you back to us some day and that we will have glorious times yet."

The last letter to Dr. Mott, in which mention is made of the Russian Movement, is dated as late as September 29, 1919—a week before Paul Nicolay's death. It sounds like the commander's last look over the death-strewn battle ground, the husbandman's last wandering through his devastated fields; and yet we are conscious throughout that it was not written by one "who has lost all hope." We quote it in entirety: [1]

"Dear Dr. Mott: Yesterday, Sept. 28th, I received two letters from you, dated September 1, and September 3, 1919, containing a request for information concerning the new Directory, and the usual string of questions sent annually to the Federation Movements.

"The present state of anarchy in Russia makes all names and addresses completely unreliable. I do not know if our headquarters in Petrograd (B. Konuschennaja 8, Lodg. 14) are still existent, or if they have been sacked by the Bolsheviks. There have been so many general massacres in Kieff that I do not know if Prof. S., Mme. O., and Miss K., are alive or dead.

[1] Quoted from the original English letter.

Nor have I news from Miss S. Miss Bréchet is in Finland, near Mustamaki Station, and M. is teaching and doing evangelistic work in the town of Samara on the Volga. Mr. G. has, I believe, returned to America.

"I suppose you will put a notice in the Directory somewhat like this: 'Owing to the conditions of anarchy still reigning in Russia, no addresses can be printed this year.'"

"Concerning the activity of our associations, no answer to the given questions can be sent. When your very life is in danger the activity of an association, as such, must temporarily cease. There can be no question of 'publication work,' 'conferences,' 'training leaders,' etc. But we know that a religious awakening is taking place in several provinces in Russia, that our scattered members are in several towns actively holding meetings which are overcrowded, and that the attitude of the educated classes and of the Russian clergy has completely changed and has become most favourably disposed. Great openings are likely in those centres whence the Bolsheviks will have been expelled.

"You see, dear Mr. Mott, it's only poor stuff I can communicate this year, but it is darkest before dawn, and Christ's Kingdom is a Kingdom which cannot be destroyed. Dan. 7 : 14."

This was the last which the founder of the Russian Student Movement wrote about his darling—the child of his sorrows—to this great leader of the World Federation. Simply and positively he lays before him facts which might have brought many to despair, without one word of complaint, without one thought for himself. It looked as if the battle waged for ten years would result in very little. The structure newly erected seemed about to crumble. Health, strength, possible personal gains were sacrificed for a cause whose future was veiled by the dense darkness of complete uncertainty. Of all this Paul Nicolay said never a word. He knew that the grain of wheat must fall into the ground and die if it shall bring forth fruit. It is easy to understand what was behind his quiet, manly trust when we recall some words once uttered by him in an address on partaking in the sufferings of Christ:

"Can it be that we, when one day we shall stand on the brink of eternity and look back over our lives, will in any way regret *what we have had the privilege* of suffering for His sake, but will not these very remembrances be the most precious of any in our lives, our greatest honour and praise? The Lord will see that *our affliction, which is short and easy, shall prepare for us an eternal measure of glory.*"

When Paul Nicolay wrote his last letter to Dr. Mott he stood on the brink of eternity. We who have been permitted to survive him know that the grain of wheat has borne fruit, that his work was not destroyed. The Russian Student Christian Movement continues to exist in starving Russian cities and towns, behind the walls of Russian prisons, and in all places in Europe where Russian student communities may be found. Paul Nicolay's disciples and fellow-workers remain at their posts among their suffering countrymen, ready to serve and to help, and when the night is darkest they turn their gaze to where his was directed at the last— towards the dawning of the day.

CHAPTER VI

In Work for the World's Student Christian Federation

"THOSE who were present at the conference of the World's Student Christian Federation in 1900 will surely recall a slim man with deep, dark eyes, who had little to say at the discussions, but whose words whether spoken in public or private conversation left a deep impression of spirituality and earnestness."

With these words Dr. Karl Fries begins an article in memory of Paul Nicolay in the "Student World," the organ of the World's Student Christian Federation.

Baron Nicolay's work was, as we know, not limited to those countries—Russia and Finland—where were his homes. He represented these countries at many international student conferences, where he took his place among the speakers and was one of the most prominent men in the work itself in spite of his quiet, retiring nature; and great was the loss when he was taken from them. "Few leaders of the World's Student Christian Federation were more loved and respected than he," writes one of his friends and coworkers. He was outstanding among many more brilliantly intellectual and oratorically gifted men, as a man who always pointed inward, always called to mind that room with the closed door to which Christ referred His disciples, as the source of power. And his unpretentiousness, his features marked by physical suffering and the struggles of a soul became one, who among many nations, should represent the work of a sorely tried and suppressed people.

As a rule, Baron Nicolay enjoyed the World Federation conferences where he met many congenial people. It was at these meetings that his friendship with Dr. Mott and Dr. Fries grew and was strengthened, and it was here also he met the man who was to hold one of the foremost places in his circle of friends—the American, Mr. Robert Wilder. Mr. Wilder, who had married a Norwegian, had built a home in Norway, and after he had become acquainted with Baron Nicolay the latter hardly ever travelled abroad without also visiting his friend in Veldre. Here he spent many happy days, rejoicing in the complete sympathy he found, in the marvellous beauty of nature, and in the pure air which became a veritable elixir of life to him, and which he greatly missed during the last years of his life, when the World War made all foreign travel impossible. But not even in Veldre did he give up his work, translating while here many pamphlets into Russian and writing Bible studies of his own. And when he was asked to speak to some larger or smaller group he courageously overcame his reluctance to comply with such a request, and was ready here also in his time of rest to share his inner riches.

Mr. Wilder has given a little picture, which was impressed upon his memory, of Baron Nicolay standing on the lawn by his friend's house and speaking to a group of older and younger men of the student world of England, America, Norway and Sweden. "His theme is the prophet Elijah; young and old alike are held spellbound by the pictures his words create. When he has finished, an Oxford graduate remarks: 'I have never known that there was so much of interest in the Old Testament. He makes these prophets live.'" Thus the experiences gathered in the quiet "morning watches" at Monrepos and St. Petersburg could be brought to members of the world's greatest and most religiously cultured nations, teaching them something new and worth while—simply because they were genuine.

Baron Nicolay's ability to work wherever he might be was to a great extent due to his extensive knowledge of languages, a fact which has already been referred to. He was very familiar with German and French; English became his key not only to Great Britain but also to the great student masses in countries outside of Europe, Swedish to those of Scandinavia, and Russian to the Slavic world. In all these languages he could not only read a report, but also give a religious or devotional address. As he was never in need of an interpreter his personality could be fully felt wherever he spoke. He could at the conferences, without difficulty, converse with any of the delegates, which naturally meant his both giving and receiving more at these conferences than many others could. Those of his addresses which he saw fit to publish he usually had translated into several languages, and he himself read proof for them. One of these addresses, referred to in another chapter, was "God Incarnate" ("Can an

AT LAKE MOHONK
In the foreground left to right, Mr. Wilder,
Baron Nicolay, Dr. Mott, and Dr. Ibuka

Educated, Thinking Man Believe in the Divinity of Jesus Christ?"), which was published in at least four languages (Russian, Swedish, Finnish, and English), and another which he delivered at the conference of the Federation in Oxford in 1909, "Participating in the Sufferings of Christ"—"a theme," says Dr. Fries, "that he was especially suited to speak on." One must rejoice to know that words such as these, which formed the nucleus of the addresses, could reach the Christian students of many lands. They make a deep impression wherever they are read, but how much more impressive must they not have been when first spoken by a man who had proven their reality.

"Have we entered into the service of Christ willing to offer ourselves in the way which He considers most suitable for His cause? *Amateurs do not advance His Kingdom.* The offering of life in many different ways is needed. If our field of labour is the Student Christian Movement with its great possibilities, we must not hesitate at the thought of what the fruitfulness may cost. But it is necessary absolutely to lay aside personal wishes regarding the place, the time, and manner of our work, and to hold neither money, health, nor life to be our own. It may mean leaving your country and living in the most uncongenial environment, being misunderstood, belittled, and slandered. It may also mean continued travelling, no home or perhaps very little of one, and possibly for some it may mean the sacrificing of life in a martyr's death. But for one and all it certainly means a great deal of self-sacrifice and hardship, much patience, toil and trouble, constant exertions in arranging and planning, temptations and pains, an anguish for souls, always being at the disposal of others, and experiencing many disappointments and times of great discouragement."

Paul Nicolay was not an amateur in his work for the furthering of God's Kingdom among students. This work to him was "service, not play," and he was therefore always ready to be used when and *where* his Lord willed. "Constant travelling" had for long been his lot, and the student work also brought him far afield. Besides the conferences of the World's Student Christian Federation at Versailles and Oxford he attended similar gatherings in many parts of Europe; in Sorö (Denmark) 1902, Zeist (Holland) 1905, and Constantinople in 1911, and also meetings in Scandinavia in Lecko 1901, Sorö 1903, and Lillehammer in 1912—here primarily as a delegate from Finland. Even beyond the boundaries of his own continent did his calling lead him. In 1907 he was present at the World's Conference in Tokio, and in 1913 at Lake Mohonk in the United States. In these journeys, weak as he was, he had occasion to experience many of the inconveniences of travel. But as Eichendorff expresses it in his famous song: "Wem Gott will rechte Gunst erweisen, den schickt er in die weite Welt," he realised something of the joy of knowing that the horizon of his knowledge and experience was expanding in a practical way. Notes in his diary tell of the journeys to Japan and America, and a passing glance at what was experienced and accomplished by Baron Nicolay on these trips may be of interest.

On March 4, 1907, Baron Nicolay started for Japan. He was still weak from an attack of influenza, an illness which he gradually began to regard as a necessary prelude to a missionary journey—and such this might be considered, since the conference in Tokio was to be followed by an evangelistic campaign in different parts of Japan. In Moscow he was joined by two delegates from Holland and one from South Africa, and there he acted as their guide. The long train journey was very tiring, but the trip on the steamer along the beautiful Angora river was wonderful. On the 20th of March the travellers reached Vladivostok where they had their first glimpse of the motley crowds of the East.

They had most beautiful weather on the trip on board the "Mongolia," and reached Japan on March 22d. At Kioto the delegates were met by an American Missionary, who entertained them with great hospitality and showed them the sights of the city, where a heathen festival was being celebrated and great crowds were in commotion. In Kioto Baron Nicolay observed—what he found to be true throughout his whole visit to Japan—the absence of "crying children and quarrelling or swearing youths." Cleanliness, order, and great politeness are apparent everywhere. "Jovial and yet refined," Baron Nicolay calls the Japanese, and the costumes so artistic in shape and colour made the appearance of the crowds very attractive.

From Kioto the Student representatives journeyed to Kobe where they saw the new university and the orphanage, whose matron, Mrs. Neesima, served "the ceremonial tea." It was amusing to see "forty little Japanese youngsters together" in the children's garden. But this did not complete the round of the city, for they had also to visit a large factory of Delft ware and the magnificent Chion temple. Baron Nicolay described the visit in these characteristic words: "I can't go into a heathen temple again, it stirs me up to have to take off my hat, and it hurts me to see this idolatry." God was to Paul Nicolay far too much of a reality to permit his watching a form of worship which seemed misdirected and false with the cold interest of an observer or with æsthetic pleasure. To have to show reverence to what was unworthy was repulsive to him, and he preferred to avoid every situation where anything of the kind might be a necessity.

From there they went to Kodzu, where Baron Nicolay partook for the first time of a truly Japanese meal served by four young Japanese girls and eaten in a squatting position with chopsticks. By electric train they then continued their journey to Youmato, and from there by foot to Mianoshito. They met with a slight snow storm and Baron Nicolay insists that the "poor Japanese shivered like butterflies in the cold." But the scenery all the way was beautiful, and especially the sight of the famous Fujiyama appealed to the travellers.

As they neared Tokio Baron Nicolay began to think more seriously about the approaching conference, which had at first been somewhat supplanted by the many external impressions. He sought to be alone with God, and rejoiced in fellowship with men who were familiar with the conditions and the people, and from whom he had occasion to learn something of the way in which it would be best to speak to Japanese students. A Missionary, whose advice he sought, emphasised the need for centring all the preaching around the person of Christ.

After a delay at Nikko for a committee meeting, Baron Nicolay finally went to Tokio where the work was to begin in earnest. When he was scheduled to speak on "The Student's Need of a Savior" in the Central Methodist Church, he suffered from a piercing headache, and wondered how he should be able to give his first address to non-Christian students in this condition. But he found the right words, spoke of students' discontent with life, of the sin and the interests which ensnare the soul, and illustrated all with examples from St. Petersburg, which he later found might have been applied to many of the five hundred Japanese in the audience. His second address, on "The Holy Scriptures and the Christian Life," seemed in the eyes of the speaker to be "a lesson in how *not* to speak." "Many thanked me, but I felt my unworthiness." Dr. Fries said of the address in question that it "plainly testified of a deep and comprehensive experience," and as it now appears in print it gives a strikingly clear picture of Paul Nicolay's relation to the Bible as to one of the springs of life. Although Baron Nicolay during his visit to Japan, as in other places, was seldom satisfied with himself, he rejoiced in the experiences he had. "It was worth the trouble of taking such a long journey to experience a time like this."

At the close of the conference he travelled with Dr. and Mrs. Fries to Sendai, Fukushima, and Yamagata, a tour planned by the conference leaders for the purpose of reaching the large student masses at these centres. In Fukushima a series of talks was given in the town hall, opened for this purpose, to about three hundred young men and women between sixteen and twenty years of age. Here Baron Nicolay spoke on Christianity's influence on character, again making use of the rich experience he had gained through fellowship with Russian students. That evening a farewell meeting was held in the church where every one squatted on mats. The young people were asked if there were any among them who, with the knowledge they now had of what Christianity is, wanted to become Christians. To the joy and amazement of the evangelists seventy-eight arose. Their names and addresses were later given to the five Japanese pastors who were in charge of the congregations in the city, where no Western Missionary was stationed. Dr. Fries later received from one of the seventy-eight a number of letters in which he first expressed his gratitude for the meetings through which a deep love for Christ had been kindled in his heart, later asked a great number of questions, and finally informed him to his great joy that he had by baptism been received into a Christian church.

Dr. Fries, who described the evangelistic tour, has also told of the many and encouraging memories preserved from these days with Paul Nicolay. "His considerateness and zeal, fired by a holy devotion, his unchangeable honesty, his wisdom and fine sensibilities, all helped to make him a most agreeable co-worker and an exceptionally valuable spiritual leader."

On the 12th of April Baron Nicolay, with the Japanese Professor Hierajama as interpreter, went to a town where he spoke on I Tim. 1 : 15,[1] and at a mass meeting in the evening on the theme: "Love, peace and joy." In Yamagata, the goal of the journey, the Europeans were met by a missionary who brought them to a hotel for a banquet which the mayor of the town had arranged in their honour. Here, writes Baron Nicolay, there was "European food, besides the Japanese which is terrible." The meetings were held in a government hall. Paul Nicolay was now given the opportunity to speak on a theme more in his line than any other, a personal relation to a personal God as the first essential for the development of character, and he felt that he was able to do it "with power." At other times he felt in Japan, as in Russia, that he must "bleed to bless." Once before rising to give an address he asks himself: "Must I always be in anguish before I speak, and not know what I shall say?" And one day when scheduled to speak three times he is long uncertain as to the subjects for *two* of his addresses. But he was accustomed to difficulties of this kind, and the time spent in Japan was to him one of inward growth and spiritual development.

On April 19th, with a very heavy sea, he left Tokio on the return journey. This journey proved to be quite an adventurous one with the fear of a threatened attack by robbers on the railway trip. But all went well, and on the 6th of May Baron Nicolay was home again in St. Petersburg. He did, however, as after the trip to Siberia in 1901, not allow himself any rest, but by May 28th was already in Dorpat where an attempt

[1] "This is a faithful saying, and worthy of all acceptation, that Christ Jesus came into the world to save sinners; of whom I am chief."

was being made to establish a branch of the Movement.

Baron Nicolay's presence at the conference in America in 1913 is of special interest on account of its being the last international conference he ever attended, and the last to be held before the breaking out of the World War. He had the joy of having with him on this trip several co-workers and members of the Movement in Russia, among whom was Mme. O., so often mentioned in his letters to Dr. Mott. He landed in New York at the end of May, going a few days later to attend a joint committee meeting at Princeton (New Jersey), where he experienced one of the greatest moments of his life. The Russian Student Christian Movement, which had come into existence in the autumn of 1912, was now admitted as a fully qualified member into the World's Federation. Not Baron Nicolay alone, but all who were present on that occasion, felt the deep significance of the event, and there was a solemn prayer of thanksgiving for the blessing that had come to the work in Russia. Another impressive moment for the delegates at Princeton was the unveiling of a monument in memory of the founding of the American Student Y. M. C. A., which they were invited to attend.

The conference itself was held at Lake Mohonk, in an extremely beautiful part of the country. Here Dr. K. Ibuka of Japan was elected chairman and Paul Nicolay vice-chairman—an honour which told of the reputation he enjoyed, but to which he paid little attention. Of the addresses which were given, Baron Nicolay singles out especially a brilliant speech by Dr.

Charles Grauss on the influence of France and a deep sermon by Bishop Brent of the Philippines. His own and Mme. O.'s accounts of the condition and needs of the Russian Student Movement aroused great interest on the part of the delegates. The sense of international brotherhood was very strongly felt here "on the mountain top." "Like our Master we saw all the kingdoms of the world and all their glory—and the glory of a consecrated life, given over to be made of worth in God's Kingdom," said an American professor at the close of the Conference.

After the Conference was officially over an excursion trip was taken to Niagara Falls whose great power deeply impressed Baron Nicolay. They travelled by way of Buffalo to Williamsport and Eaglesmere, where a summer conference was being held. In the evening Baron Nicolay was again given the opportunity to speak on Russia, and once more the students were enthused by the opportunities for work in that vast, mysterious and, to so many, unknown land of the East.

At Northfield the delegation was asked to remain for the athletic stunts, without seeing which a visit to America could hardly be considered complete. The representatives of the different countries had by now become well acquainted, felt at home in each other's company, and spent many happy hours together. The childlike spirit of joy which was Paul Nicolay's, when he would at times "let himself go," now expressed itself in an original way. At an evening gathering all the European delegates marched to the platform and he explained that their choir would now render "the concert of Europe." This was done by every member of the choir singing loudly and at the same time the national anthem of his own country—a good-natured satire, but with a prophetical significance more dreadful than could be dreamed. When the World War broke out in the following year, with its most jarring mental discord, the violent outbreak of every people's national egoism, many who had been at Northfield looked sadly back on what had then seemed but an innocent joke. And especially did he, who had organised the play that evening, who says of the visit to America that "such a gathering was like a foretaste of heaven," and who rejoiced in the glorious and trustful relation which can exist between nations when sanctified by the spirit of Christ. How happy he would have been had he been permitted to live long enough to see how the inner unity of the Student Christian Federation was affected less by the World War than that of any other international union.

By reason of his great knowledge of languages Baron Nicolay became of invaluable service to the World's Federation in its international intercourse. He was even able to help by interpreting for some of the representatives of the smaller nations. Mr. Wilder tells in the "Student World" of a meeting in Austria, where the audience represented *eighteen* universities and *thirteen* nationalities, how a Bulgarian student expressed his desire to speak, but did not see how this could be possible as he knew no language but his own. Immediately Paul Nicolay declared his willingness to interpret him into German, thus overcoming a situation which might have been painful. Although Baron Nicolay's knowledge of Bulgarian can

not have been great, he was at least able by his mastery
of one Slavic language—Russian—and his unique understanding of the Slavic nature to form a connecting
link between the student world of the Balkan States
and Western Europe.

In the beginning of 1911 he travelled with Dr. Mott
to Switzerland where he was able in several places to
interpret for him, and where he sought to organise
Bible groups among the many Slavic students residing
there. In the same year he was asked to pave the way
in Sofia, Belgrade and Bucharest for a visit by Dr.
Mott. This was no easy task, for he had here to work
for a completely new idea with innumerable prejudices
to overcome, to probe the unfathomable attitude of the
Slavic authorities, and to secure the co-operation of
trustworthy men who would also be respected in the student world. But Paul Nicolay, due to his vast experience and his habit of facing similar difficulties, was the
right man for the task. Some excerpts from a letter
to Dr. Mott will suffice to show how he undertook
the work in the Balkan States with the same quiet consideration and sound practical judgment as in Russia.
From Sofia on February 27th he writes: [1]

"This afternoon I intend to leave for Belgrade, and
want to let you know something of my impressions.
On the whole they are good and I find Sofia a very
hopeful place. . . .

"The rector, it is true, cancels his former invitation
that you should come as guest of the University, but
this is not on account of unfriendliness or fear of

[1] Quoted from the original English letter.

Protestant propaganda, but, as he candidly told me, he is afraid of the students. Another prominent and influential professor also finds that the students have such an exaggerated sense of independence, that they would resent it if professors meddled with their concerns. Anyhow all the professors I spoke with are very ready to invite you to a cup of tea and will be glad to have a talk with you. Professor Schismanoff is a keyman, very intelligent and friendly, who has studied Christianity from a historical and sociological point of view *only,* and expressed his wish to have a deeper talk with you. It would be well worth while.

"The rector definitely promised to give you the largest auditorium in the University. I gave him your letter and read to him the contents of the introduction for the Minister of Public Instruction. . . .

"I had a very good impression of Mr. B., a nice, teachable, intelligent, quiet, Christian man of business, serving in a bank and belonging to no church. Among the students who are members of the Y. M. C. A. I found some very fine men—Mr. N. A., a real student, nominally a member of the Greek Orthodox Church, but quite evangelical; Mr. S. V., an intelligent gentlemanly fellow and devoted Christian. I had no difficulty whatever to convince these men of the absolute necessity of avoiding all appearances even of Protestant propaganda in our work, to prepare for your arrival on strictly interdenominational lines and by no means under even the shadow of the flag of the Y. M. C. A. They have by experience learned that it is hopeless to work differently, and themselves expressed the wish to form a student group according to our principles independent of the Y. M. C. A. I advised them not to form any new organisation before your arrival, but to form Student Bible Circles now among themselves, and to use our hand-book, so as to have some training for later when you will have had your lectures.

". . . They would like one address to be on 'Science and Religion.' Maybe some of the workers like Miss Rouse or Wilder should stay on after your departure to follow up. . . . Concerning a translator, I think it would be better if a good translator could be found to translate into Bulgarian, rather than my translating into Russian, which is more or less understood by all students, but not perfectly.

"They say that the Queen is much interested in Christian work and would possibly wish to see you, but that an interview with royalty would spoil your influence with students. . . .

"Concerning the irreligiousness of the students and their indifference to religious subjects, I fancy they will come, though out of curiosity, like they do in other places, if only the advertising is well carried out and the time chosen when they are in town. One of the professors told me that the students want an address to be clear, to the point, giving palpable facts and practical reasons for joining a movement like ours, and also clear indications of what would be expected of them. They are suspicious of hidden motives and must be convinced that we have none."

From Belgrade, where Baron Nicolay found "a man sent from God" ready to help in every way, he writes as follows: [1]

"The rector took matters seriously when I showed

[1] Quoted from the original English letter.

him the attitude of the Swiss professors and especially the letter to the Minister of Public Instruction. He offers the large hall of the University. I saw several other professors, of whom Professor Marco Lecco showed genuine interest and asked for literature in German. . . . The spiritual condition is such that I only could tell Mrs. C. that it is darkest before dawn.

"I advised them, besides three meetings with students, to give you one conversazione with professors and one meeting for thoughtful townspeople. You will have to pitch into them and tell them that religion is not yet dead and done for, as they imagine."

In Bucharest Baron Nicolay found every one occupied with the Parliamentary elections—the Minister, the rector, all away electioneering. He describes a visit to the archimandrite whom he found friendly but noncommittal, and who sent him to a Christian professor of medicine who was suffering from influenza, and continues:[1]

"I met several times the influential student Mr. I., whom Miss Rouse mentions, but he, too, is reserved. I could not quite believe it at first, but it seems that Mr. Adeney is right in saying that just at present everybody is deadly afraid of 'propaganda,' especially Roman Catholic, but also Protestant. . . . I found out that the first step to be taken was to begin at the top and see the Minister of Public Instruction. Yesterday I saw his secretary and found him a nice, serious man, who would be in sympathy with influencing the students in a *moral* way. . . . To-day I met his Excel-

[1] Quoted from the original English letter.

lency the Minister, who, though personally I believe quite indifferent to the matter, was exceedingly polite, gave his consent, promised a hall, and even said he would be happy to hear you himself. So now the way is opened and to-morrow I am to meet the Rector and decide about a committee. I shall ask that one student from each faculty be on it, in hopes that Mr. I. will be appointed one of them, being a prominent man, but I may not mention his name so as not to harm him. . . . To the secretary and to the Minister I have said nothing about the Federation, but only about your *lectures*. . . . The main point to aim at is to give you the chance of addressing the students. All the rest will follow naturally, I hope."

His impression of his visit to Bucharest was not favourable, and Baron Nicolay closes his letter by saying, "Much prayer is needed to secure your success in these Balkan States." When a couple of months later Dr. Mott, accompanied by Baron Nicolay, lectured in the places "prepared" he seemed indeed to be facing great obstacles—especially in Belgrade where, during his final address, the socialists began to demonstrate, to cry out, whistle, and knock over chairs. Nevertheless, the foundations were laid for a growing work. Most encouraging were the results in Sofia, where the admonitions from Belgrade to break up the meetings were of no avail, and where not even Dr. Mott's audience with the Queen could dissolve the good impression he had made.

The following year the Balkan lands were visited by Sherwood Eddy, whose addresses resulted in great

progress. Baron Nicolay had expected to accompany
him there, but did not have to do so as Eddy found
another companion. But he did not forget the field
where he had prepared the way, but followed the work
with keen interest, and especially with much prayer.
One of the great joys of his life was a letter received
in the summer of 1919 from a Bulgarian student who
had formerly belonged to the Kieff branch of the Russian Movement, and who now wrote of the successful
spiritual work he was able to carry on in Sofia. He
held also an official position in the capital of his country, and had thus "the opportunity now and again of
defending the addresses of good Christian speakers."
Here Baron Nicolay could see the fruit of his labour
which consisted, according to Dr. Mott, in "educating
the educators and leaders of the people." Radiantly
he showed his friend Baron Henrik Wrede, who visited him during his last illness, these precious words
which testified to how mighty was the Lord of the
Harvest even where the prospects seemed least promising.

In this sphere also Paul Nicolay was survived by his
work. One of those now working in the Slavic lands,
Mrs. W. J. Rose of Canada, has recently said that
these countries have never been so open to the influence of the Gospel as at the present time, and in connection with this she speaks of Paul Nicolay, whom she
met at a conference at Ligotka in Silesia in 1914, and
whose influence she deeply values. The characteristics
of his personality which she depicts will perhaps sum
up better than anything else what it was that deter-

mined his position within the World's Student Christian Federation:[1]

"The gentleness of Baron Nicolay made a deep impression on the Slav students at our Federation Conference in Ligotka, 1914. We of the Western World are apt to underestimate the value of this quality—one of the cluster of the fruits of the Holy Spirit. The voice of God is not always in the wind and in thunder, but in the stillness. And it was the repose of this servant of Christ, the calm faith in Gōd that made him so beloved by us all. Surely in these days of nervous haste, impatience, and striving, the personality of Baron Nicolay should be an inspiration for us. Surely we too will gain more in strength if we cease our rushing and withdraw into the stillness to seek God, by whom alone wisdom and power for our tasks can be given. If the man, whose personality is for us a precious memory, could speak to us to-day, would he not point out this communion with God as the source of all joy and healing for the wounds made by the war?"

[1] Quoted from the original English account by Mrs. Rose.

CHAPTER VII

In Finland

*C*ITIZEN *of the World* is a term which might be
justly applied to such a man as was Paul Nicolay.
The whole world was his sphere of service, all people
who needed help on their way to Christ were his people.
That country which seemed to need him most was Russia, and to her he devoted his best strength and the
greater portion of his time. Yet he was not entirely
rooted there. We have seen how England was the
land of his longings; but it was too far away. There
was, however, one country which gradually came to be
his home, where he could work unhindered, where love
and sympathy became his portion, a land which through
his birth-right he might even call his own. That land
was Finland.

Paul Nicolay was born a Finnish Baron and heir
to an estate on Finnish soil. By attending Parliament
he had learned to know the educated class, and by visits
to Monrepos and missionary work on the coast her
country population. He had acquired both of the languages of the land and, though speaking neither of
them quite correctly, could easily make himself understood in Finnish, and in Swedish readily give voice to
his deepest thoughts. The changing fate of Finland
never left him untouched, his heart bled when her
people suffered and he, the submissive and self-con-

trolled, would inwardly rebel against the blows aimed at her independence. During the "Bobrikoff" period of suppression—those distressful years—entries often occur in his diary similar to these: "A terrible day for Finland!" "I hope they will not promulgate. It would be too mean." Or again, "New authority for the Governor General to send into exile! Such murderous thoughts beset me." Yes, he, who usually stood apart from all politics, willingly put himself at the disposal of his Finnish friends to gain information on a situation or plead for justice in Finland in influential Russian circles.

In Evy Fogelberg's book "The Prisoners' Friend" we find an account of a visit made by Mathilda Wrede, in his company, in 1899 to the Metropolitan Antony. Baron Nicolay manifested on this occasion his characteristic gentle firmness. When the "Metropolitan" objected to a request put to him by saying that "he had no influence," Paul Nicolay replied: "Every honest man has some influence, and he who knows the right and does not do it, for him it is sin." Baron Henrik Wrede tells of another incident in which Paul Nicolay championed the cause of Finland and justice. When his friend Maximovsky had been assigned the task of assisting in recasting Finland's penal law, he strove hard to influence him to an attitude favourable to his country. And if any of his Finnish friends were in danger, Paul Nicolay was always the first turned to in order to disentangle if possible the case. However busy he might be and however poor his health, he was always ready to help.

Paul Nicolay loved Finland's legal orderliness, he

loved Finland's people—"our beloved Finnish people" he often called them and never differentiated between the Swedish and Finnish Finlanders, for to him such a distinction did not exist. He loved the atmosphere of peace and order which prevailed before the war in the land. But most of all he loved Finland's students.

Madame af Forselles has told how Paul Nicolay in January of 1901, for the first time apart from summer conferences at Åbo, was prevailed on to address a group of Finnish students of both sexes, and how in his discouragement he afterward exclaimed: "What a fool you have made of me!" and added, "Never again will I speak to students." Baron Nicolay very soon learned the truth of the saying "never say never," for he was often to speak to students, including Finnish students, and with unusually great success. And the words he uttered that day at the home of Madame af Forselles— simple, direct words on the meaning of the Cross of Christ—were never forgotten by those who heard him, and became a worth-while introduction to his future work.

Baron Nicolay's contribution to the summer conference at Åbo in 1900 has already been mentioned. He was present at nearly all similar conferences in the future and was as a matter of course always made a member of the committees of arrangement. When the programme was first drawn up he wrote lengthy letters to the secretaries of the Student Christian Movement with explicit replies to all the questions which were asked of him. He advised on the place of meeting, the suitability of proposed speakers, subjects for addresses, and many other details—but he never demanded nor expected that all these suggestions be followed. Nothing could illustrate better than these letters Paul Nicolay's great and genuine humility. He wrote to the inexperienced young people who were in the work of the Movement as if to complete equals, and always respected their point of view. If things did not go as he had wished, if his "companions" in the Movement opposed some of his suggestions, he usually assumed that God had intended the matter to take such a turn. But he never refused to share his experiences, whether they might apply to summer conferences, selection of office holders, lectures, work of Bible groups, or anything else.

At the conferences themselves Baron Nicolay usually gave several addresses, often being asked for the opening or closing address of the conference. But he also took a much more active part, as he was the inspirational and leading spiritual force. These were never allowed to degenerate into excursions or summer festivals, but they must be prepared for and supported by much prayer, and all the converted students be reminded of their responsibility to their seeking companions. One of his favourite similes was that God does not want Christians to be like sponges, merely absorbing the Water of Life, seeking sanctification and spiritual deepening for themselves, and never giving anything. The joy of youth must come to its own, and here as at the Russian conferences Baron Nicolay could be the gladdest of the glad—but never in a way that might efface his real purpose, the winning of souls for Christ. Those who have been with him recall how often a conversation on everyday things would gradually take on a serious tone, until he would interrupt it with a quiet: "Let us now put these thoughts into the form of prayer."

The summer days spent in a beautiful place became days of refreshment to him. He was at home with Finland's students, and to them he became a true friend and perhaps more of an authority than he himself might have wished. As the train, approaching the place where the summer conference was to meet, gradually filled with young Finnish students in white caps, his face lit up and great was his joy when the chorus struck up some conference hymn: "Det är ett kosteligt ting" (It is a precious thing), or "Om dig, Om dig, O Jesu, vill jag sjunga" (Of Thee, of Thee, oh, Jesus, will I sing). He was not musical nor a judge of sacred music, but he loved these hymns. He found the self-reliant freshness of youth especially restful after the nervous strain of Russia. And the young people thronged around him—"Baron Nicolay," "Uncle Paul" —and nothing was as it should be unless he were along. To hear his gentle cheerful voice say in greeting, "God dag, god dag, kära van" (Good day, good day, dear friend) with the familiar burr in "kära," to catch sight of the inevitable sport cap, which would disappear into the pocket of his grey coat, gave to every one immediately the feeling of being at home.

And in the days that followed "Baron" remained, despite his modest and almost shy manner, the central figure at the conference. His Bible studies on such men as Elijah, Jacob, or Paul, or on a subject like "The Power of Faith" always contained some practical truths which etched themselves into the memory, never to be forgotten. What a new significance came to the story of Jacob, so hard to understand, when it was characterised as the account of "God's leading and training of a man with a *considerably* (in Baron Nicolay's mouth "greatly") complex and difficult character," and how the second chapter of the Sermon on the Mount was clarified, when it was pointed out that it stressed throughout the need for "truth in the inward parts." [1] Striking was his interpretation of Matt. 5 : 22—"Antipathy is hatred." And how his talks went home with their personal appeal to every conscience, without pathos or presumption! "But your and my attitude to Him must be genuine in all things"—these words typify all Baron Nicolay's statements. They were in his eyes the first condition for an approach to Christ, and he never wearied of pointing this out, nor did any grow weary of listening to it.

Significant is a remark of quite a young boy at the Ilmajoki Conference, the last ever attended by Baron Nicolay. When some one asked the youth which of the speakers he liked best, he answered immediately "Baron Nicolay; one can't but believe what he says." The secret of his influence was just the limitless confidence he inspired, which forced all to pause before what was truth to this truthful man. Thus it was with suspense that people waited for what he would say in answer to some "question," one of those anonymous written questions which were placed in the "question box" at summer conferences to be answered by some of the older people present. The answer often con-

[1] Psalm 51 : 6.

tained practical advice of great help to the questioner,
usually references to Bible verses or a suggestion to
study a Bible narrative from a definite angle, and occasionally—if the question were peripheral in nature
—an injunction to let it alone and concentrate on the
essentials. Very often the answer struck a weak spot
in the conscience of the asker, forcing him to look at
himself in a new light. But it always came like a
helping hand from an experienced comrade-in-arms,
and never as an indisputable oracle nor something complete which could be received with no effort on one's
own part. A man must, he felt, be converted, "not to
us, nor to our dogmatic views, but to a personal experience of the truth."

As Shepherd of Men's Souls Paul Nicolay was also
known within our Student Christian Movement. He
was never happier than when some one came to talk
with him about his spiritual difficulties, as was often
the case at summer conferences as well as during his
visits to Helsingfors. In this way he opened up for
many young seekers the way to a personal Christianity, by showing them that a great many questions could
at first be left unanswered if only the conscience were
gripped by Christ and the *will* yielded to Him. He,
whose life of faith was so simple and complete, dis-
played a wonderful sympathy even for those who were
troubled by rather unusual doubts. Typical in every
respect of Paul Nicolay is a letter to such a young
person who informed him that she did not feel she
could work with other Christians, as she did not know
whether her beliefs agreed in the main with theirs—
the atoning power of Christ still being a concept for-

eign to her. The letter goes to the heart of the matter.

"I remember what it has cost me spiritually to 'stand on my own feet,' to be 'under the law of Christ,' but free from 'the law of men.' I wanted to be faithful and conscientious in my relation to God and His Word, but without letting men put their stamp on me, forcing me to imitate them in dogma or phraseology. . . . To me 'Christ in me' has meant more than 'Christ for me,' as my experience has been more along that line. That does not mean that the other concept is unnecessary or superfluous. He reveals Himself to one person more from one angle, to another from another, and we gradually realise that the different ways do not contradict but rather complement each other.

"But what makes you think that you must feel isolated among Christians? He who says of Christ 'my Lord and my God,' he is certainly a Christian. It is wonderful that the Christians' unity does not consist in unity of forms and expressions, but in the unity of the spirit. Christ loves his flowers, not wanting them to imitate each other but that each in his own special way should try to resemble Him—that there might be 'unity in diversity.' 'One is your Master—Christ,' not men. That makes us *free,* but *yielded* to Christ. As long as you serve Him humbly and with a good conscience you need not worry about the future and that you may have to stand alone. All somewhat mature Christians must come to recognise your right to independence under the guidance of Christ."

The writer seemed to know just how to place himself in the position of the questioner to get the right point of view on her special difficulties. How circumspect and yet how firm was his hold on the young soul. His clear conception of every soul's right to individual development, his certainty that "God wants *originals* and *not copies*," was of great value in his intercourse with students. And what a clear and beautiful picture he unconsciously gives of himself, free but yielded, the bondservant of Christ, but of no one else.

It is not strange that Paul Nicolay's personal influence on the Finnish students was great, and became his foremost contribution to our Student Christian Movement. He became unconsciously, to many of the students, an ideal or at least a stirring example. The educational influence he exerted on the members of the Movement who came into touch with him can hardly be overestimated. Not with words alone, but still more forcibly with his life did he emphasise the central things. He sought for inner worth alone, and moved among these young people, who were often from small and simple homes, as artlessly and naturally as he would in the salon of a prince, never affectedly courteous but always friendly and helpful to the very youngest, always self-controlled and patient. Thus he revealed to many the meaning of true culture of the soul, its aversion to all self-sufficiency, insolent demanding of one's own right, and selfish effeminacy in every form. To see "our Baron"—"paronimme"—on his way to a summer conference, rise and offer his seat to some one or, in the most natural way, load himself with the luggage of another, had a greater

effect than many sermons on the young men who were
with him.

One who had been with Paul Nicolay describes an
event which was ineffaceably engraved on his memory. Baron Nicolay was standing outside the student
building in Helsingfors when the throng at the tramway cars was at its worst, trying to find room in one
of them. People elbowed their way forward, as is
the way of the world. By the Baron's side stood a
simple labourer's wife who had great difficulty in getting into the car, for others who were stronger kept
jostling her aside. Finally Baron Nicolay, patiently
awaiting his own turn, raised his gentle voice in her
cause: "Be considerate of this lady!" "That voice
came as from another world," wrote the one who told
of the event, "a world which is governed by the laws
of righteousness, which protect the rights of the small
and the weak." Seldom did Baron Nicolay speak of
social injustice, and reluctantly did he discuss political
questions with the students. But by giving them an
example in nobility of heart, he likewise gave them a
glimpse into the spirit of true democracy.

Gentle tactfulness characterised Baron Nicolay, and
was advocated by him. When he encouraged "personal work" for the winning of souls he often added,
"Naturally we must be tactful." In this respect as in
others he felt we should go in Jesus' footsteps; He
knocks at the door of our heart, but He does not violently break his way in, He is far too tactful for that;
He waits for us to open for Him. But as a flag over
a consulate shows to the citizens of a country where
they may find their official representative, so we should

always show our colors that those who long for Christian fellowship or guidance may without hesitation turn to us. This was then his final solution of the "problem of witnessing," which had troubled him so much in his youth.

Baron Nicolay himself was always ready to help any who needed him by word or deed. Nothing which might serve God's Kingdom was trivial in his sight, and he always practised a strict fidelity even in the smallest things. Never wittingly did he leave a letter unanswered, never missed an appointment, never forgot what had been entrusted to him. His punctuality was phenomenal, and he likewise expected others to be punctual in their relationships with him. In this matter the Finnish students must have caused him many bitter disappointments. To him punctuality was one phase of honesty—his yea must always be yea, and his nay, nay. If he were ever forced to revoke a promise he was deeply grieved. Thus he once writes when he cannot find a subject for a message: "I am willing during the next days even by 'prayer and fasting' to seek a message from God; but what if it should not come? Then there would be no alternative but to go on strike and let P. give his address alone, and never show myself in the Movement rooms again after having fooled you in such a way." There is severe self-reproach behind these half-facetious words.

It was always a great day for the members of the Movement when Baron Nicolay came to Helsingfors, and it seemed every time as if he brought with him an invigorating breath of air, however "dry and exhausted" he often felt himself to be. It was easier to pray and work when he was there, and although his visits were rare—a couple of times during the academic year—the whole life of the Movement was, like the summer conferences, gradually permeated by his personality. The spirit of prayer and simple devotion which was his became predominant within the Finnish Student Christian Movement, though perhaps somewhat at the expense of the purely academic, yet as a sign of spiritual freedom and joyful willingness for work.

That the Movement could not always remain at the height where Baron Nicolay would like to see it, that he was far from always satisfied with its activities, is natural. In many of his letters we find quite severe criticism of the work, but always given by a friend and not by a fault-finder. "The Finnish Movement is passing through a period of stagnation; you ought to come here," he might, for example, write to his friend Mr. Wilder.

It was just these times of standing still which troubled him most, the periods when the growth of the Movement seemed checked. By growth he might mean external development, new victories in the student world, and he felt it important for the Movement never to forget its *missionary* task. But above all he sought the inner spiritual development. After the summer conference at Ilmajoki, which satisfied him in the main, he writes in his diary about the Movement itself: "How it has grown in quantity, but hardly in quality." As in Russia, he stressed here also the importance of a nucleus of live Christians within the Movement to give colour to its activity. And if he felt that its inner life seemed threatened, that the salt was about to lose its savour, he was the first to raise a voice of warning. At his suggestion, so-called "retreats" had begun to be organised in Finland in 1913. At these, small groups of Movement members met in quiet rural spots to seek deeper consecration and to confer on the work. None of those who had responsibility in regard to the spiritual work of the Movement, and thus for the souls of others, should be satisfied with the knowledge of being converted and saved, but they must, with never diminishing intensity, press onward along the path of *sanctification*.

One member of the Movement jotted down in his note-book some words spoken by Baron Nicolay in an address on February 6, 1914, which were engraved in the memory of many: "Our highest task is to glorify God by our conduct." In connection with this Baron Nicolay mentioned some "precious stones" worthy of possession: patience which may be quite hard to obtain, gentleness which enables the mind of its owner to be quiet and at peace even when others grow angry and lose the equilibrium of their souls, purity even in thought life, courage which is independent of the opinion of the majority, veracity which tolerates nothing that is not perfectly true, and, finally, love even towards the uncongenial.

Such was the ideal he set up for the young people, and based on the Sermon on the Mount, "a mirror," as he liked to call it, "in which we see ourselves as we are, and as we ought to be." Towards this ideal every Christian ought to strive throughout his life, not in his own strength, but by preserving the vital touch with

God. "We must not be locomotives, but electric tram cars," he often said, aiming at just that contact. Again and again he referred students to the two great sources of power: the Bible and Prayer, to the quiet moments of eternity in "the Morning Watch." "How are you keeping the Morning Watch?" he inquired one morning of one of the members whom he met after rather a long separation, and whom he heard complaining of spiritual dearth. "Keep an iron grip on the Morning Watch," was his admonition to another of his old students, who visited him a short time before his death and who now holds a leading position in the Movement. It was like a last greeting to the whole of the Student Christian Movement. "Keep an iron grip on the Morning Watch!"—by devotion—by sanctification.

Little did Baron Nicolay himself realise how indispensable he had gradually become to the Christian Students of Finland, he had too little confidence in his own work for that. When he was invited to Helsingfors to deliver a series of lectures in the large hall of the University, or Bible Studies in the Movement rooms, he was astonished to find that people wanted to "have him." For he felt that there were so many others who might be made use of. At that time when he was afraid of being forced to "strike" on account of being unable to find a "message," he wrote further: "It is quite possible that you may have overlooked some one who God had intended should speak, and that it was not His will at all that I should speak again." And when in the spring of 1919 he was invited by the Northern Committee to speak at the Scandinavian Summer Conference held that year in Denmark, he, who had taken part several times in the past, flatly refused, mentioning in his reply a list of young speakers who "could represent Finland much better than he." But touched and gratified he was by every sign of the students' affection. When in 1914 he had to be absent from a summer conference at Åbo, the delegates of the conference sent him a greeting with a large number of signatures. In his letter of thanks he expressed surprise, and added, "God bless them all for their kindness to a 'vanha ukko' (old man). I will keep this list *as a truly valuable gift.*"

As a "vanha ukko," an "uncle" who was already a little out of the game, he often described himself in relation to the younger workers in the Movement. He was afraid of being in their way, afraid even of "not being of use at the meetings." When at the Ilmajoki Conference he did not come into as close contact with the young students as before, he remarked to Madame af Forselles with a humour touched with pathos: "Here we go around like two Olympic gods." To be placed on a pedestal was the last thing he desired. He wanted to serve students, not to be admired by them. Nevertheless, it must have been with joy that he in 1918 received a call from the Student Christian Movement in Finland to be its first honorary member. He could not fail to realise the sincere warmth which prompted this action. And what he had in reality become to the Finnish Students finds expression in the following words written after his departure:

"We feel as if we had become fatherless; but I am convinced that he will never die for any who even in

STUDENT CONFERENCE AT TAVASTEHUS, FINLAND, 1913

ON BOARD THE YACHT "LADY"

the capacity of listeners were brought within the sphere of his influence. He will always remain an encouraging and stimulating example of how God can transfigure and sanctify a life which is wholly devoted to Him."

If Paul Nicolay could have known that he had been able to reveal to the Christian students of Finland something of God's power to change and sanctify souls, it would have greatly rejoiced his heart. For that was what he had most deeply desired.

In the membership of Finland's Student Christian Movement one group has always been more strongly represented than others, the theological students. It is usually quite natural for young men, often from religious homes, who come to the University to prepare for the ministry, to join an organisation of this kind. Thus for two decades the Student Christian Movement has been to the prospective preachers and pastors, especially of the national church, a sort of practical training school through which the theoretical training of the University is afforded an active outlet. Here they have been brought into touch with educated, earnest young people of different religious trends and different ranks of society; here they have become accustomed through discussions with students of the humanities, medical and sociological students, to clarify their scientific and practical attitude to questions regarding their own religious life. When they first began to take their place as speakers and religious leaders among intellectually developed and exacting companions, they began to learn to give of their best in their work. Thus the Student Movement accomplished an important task in the service of the Church, and in this respect never has any one exerted a deeper or more lasting influence than Baron Nicolay. One who in student years heard him emphasise a personal relation to a personal God, based on perfect sincerity as the goal and purport of religion, who through fellowship with him learned the significance of such a relationship, he could never as a pastor be content to tread the old and worn-out paths of indolence or self-sufficiency, but he must strive to perform a living work in the presence of the living God. Through his work in the Movement Paul Nicolay became in his own characteristic way—working from the inside out—a reformer in church life. And towards the close of his life he was to take even a more active part in this work.

As we have already seen, Baron Nicolay seemed rather indifferent in his attitude to the church in which he was baptised. What was merely empty outward form did not attract him, and within the Lutheran Church he had seen in his childhood, and even later, external forms advance far too often at the expense of the substance. "Unconverted" pastors, who from the pulpit preached things they did not believe or which had not as yet become real to them, he always judged severely. He found their sermons unspeakably tiresome, and never made a secret of it. "Why do they go so far away to look for their subjects? Is it strange if people give up attending church?" is one remark in his diary. Baron Wrede tells of an occasion in which they both listened to a sermon of the "tiresome" kind.

When Baron Wrede remarked at the close that he was
going home to rest and "take a little nap," his friend
replied, "I have already done that"; and to the question,
when and where it had been possible, the quaint re-
sponse was, "In church." Very sharply did Baron Nicolay, at another time, speak of a pastor who prayed "not
to God, but to his congregation." An insincere emphasis
in a prayer or religious address, whether spoken in a
Lutheran Church or Free Church Chapel, always
caused him pain. He had little patience with theological subtleties, with narrow-minded dogmatism or
formalism. "I have always been a poor church
Christian, both in the Lutheran and Free Church," he
admitted in 1914. He himself, as we know, was willing to grant the individual great freedom in his relations to God as long as he was "consecrated to Christ."
Though not a follower of the radical trend in Biblical
research—"too much radical theology" was his disap-
proving verdict of one Northern Conference—he would
not deny any one the right to his own attitude in this
matter, as long as the investigator "remained humble
and was willing to be taught of God." And he maintained that no views, however orthodox, could constitute the condition for salvation. Significant is the
question he put to a person who was anxious regarding a departed friend, who had before his death pro-
fessed belief in "the modern theories": "Do you think
that we are saved through our orthodoxy?" Neither
to him was participating in any church form essential
to a relationship with God, although he held the sacraments of the church in great reverence.

The views which in his early years he found held

by Lutheran clergy were, as a rule, so completely different that a certain prejudice against the whole body was
aroused in him.   When in 1902 Baron K. A. Wrede
passed the examination for "venia concionandi," granting him the right to preach in the churches, Paul
Nicolay disapproved of the step and let his friend hear
biting remarks on it. "You may still end up as a
pastor," he said sarcastically. "If your work is of any
value it is simply because you are not a pastor, and
yet preach the Word of God."   But in time he learned
to appreciate the reason for his friend's action.   His
attitude to the Lutheran Church gradually underwent
a great change.   This was not due to the lessening of
what he required of the clergy, but to his more often
seeing pastors who met these requirements, and also to
his eyes being opened to the great place the Church as
such should have in the life of the people.

The student work in Finland contributed largely to
this change in Baron Nicolay's point of view.   He was
here brought, through his fatherly attitude to many
of the young theologians, into a more intimate relation
with that Church in which they were to work, and to
which he could no longer remain as a critical onlooker.
And at the summer conferences he also learned to know
many older pastors, among whom were many sympathetic, sincere, and unpretentious men of a totally
different type from the formal representatives of a dead
ecclesiasticism who were his dread.

While he was thus gaining a brighter outlook on the
men of the church, he was becoming to many of them
a real revelation of what might be accomplished through
good lay preachers.   And his profound knowledge of

the Bible, added to the rich experience behind his un-)
pretentious bearing, won their respect and admiration.'
At the conference at Åbo in 1900, Baron K. A. Wrede,
in the dark vestibule outside the hall where his friend
had spoken, was embraced by a pastor who evidently
mistook him for Nicolay, although the enthusiastic
pastor, on realising his mistake, amiably added: "It'll
be for Wrede then!" Even if this hearty token of
friendship failed to reach Baron Nicolay at the time,
he was later to receive many similar ones from the
Finnish pastors.

In 1905 Baron Nicolay for the first time took part
in the work of the Church, when he was prevailed upon
to hold a series of revival meetings in the City Mission
Chapel Betania in Helsingfors. The following year
he was invited with Baron Wrede to be a speaker at
the first separate conference for the edification of pastors, which was to be held at Åbo. "A strange invitation," he felt this call to be, as he regarded himself still
so far removed from the clergy and their interests.
Nevertheless he accepted the call, making a complete
success as a church speaker and gaining many new
friends among the delegates. Yet, in the following
year when he is about to take part in the meeting for
pastors in Seinojoki he asks himself: "How can I speak
to all these pastors?" And he has later many objections to offer on the organisation of the conference;
what they wanted in the spiritual realm did not seem
adequately clear, and too much time was wasted in
drinking coffee. That the purely religious values
were taken more into consideration at the future pastors' conferences was to a large measure due to the

presence of Baron Nicolay. This man, familiar with
the highest society, who had learned to use all that he
had "not as if he were using it," and who in concentrating on the affairs of the Kingdom of God could dis-
cover "wordliness" in anything as innocent in Finnish
eyes as was wasting time on drinking coffee, must by
his very personality here, as at student conferences,
have had the effect of a powerful sermon.

A wide field of activity was gradually being opened
up to Baron Nicolay in the realm of the church. To be
sure he had neither the time nor the strength to accept
all the invitations he received to speak at meetings, but
he did often speak in churches, especially in the Mission Church in Helsingfors. It was usually Baron
Wrede who tried to prevail on him to do so when he
came to Helsingfors for student work. Often he stub-
bornly resisted the attempts to entice him into a sphere
which lay "outside his circle of responsibility." But
when he had once been prevailed upon to address a
church gathering, he did his utmost here also to give
the best he had to offer. He preferred to speak to a
smaller group, but not at sewing societies or meetings
with a programme and serving of tea, for he wanted to
have his audience entirely with him. If he were
"forced" to the pulpit he usually dismissed the event in
a letter with the short but expressive word—"awful."
He did not feel himself suited to speak to a large and
mixed audience; for he preferred to know whom he
was addressing, whether they were educated people,
whether the majority were real believers or merely religiously interested. At revival meetings in the real
sense of that word he refused, in the later years of his

life, to speak. When urged to do so he always insisted
that it was not in his line to take people by storm. In
this connection he told how an Esthonian peasant
woman prophesied of him, after a dream she had, that
his work for God's Kingdom would not be sowing—
revivals—neither reaping—the joy of bringing people
to conversion—but preparation of the field in the hearts
of men, thus leading them to a fuller, more complete,
and better Christianity.

We have already seen how Baron Nicolay both sowed
and reaped. But his work in Finland was perhaps
more along the line indicated by the Esthonian woman
—at least so he himself thought—and as he grew
older he preferred to concentrate more on this type of
work, of preparing the hearts of Christians for a more
complete reception of the Master. When he addressed
a group of believers on a Biblical subject he liked to
see them with their Bibles in their hands, so that he
might in a sense be their guide through a land which
to him was so full of wonderful and undreamed-of
riches.

In order to appreciate what the Book of books was
to him, it is only necessary to open his own Swedish
Bible, so worn at the edges that one almost fears to
turn the pages. Every page, every line of it tells of
the relation which the owner of the book bore to it until
the last. Underlinings, arrows, and all kinds of marks
—a completely developed system of signs—give a remarkable appearance to the Book, and the notes in the
margin written in different languages force the reader
to pause before one verse and another. Close to a
"then" isolated by a circle and introducing a subject,

we read the words "God's time." In the seventeenth
chapter of the Gospel of John there is a line joining all
the references in which the significant word "one"
occurs, and in many places there is a comparison with
the Greek or English text. Thus we may picture how
Paul Nicolay during his daily Morning Watch and
many another hour in the course of the day sat bent
over the Book, thoroughly alert and active, as in conversation with his Lord, with his soul open to the influence of His Spirit. And we can also understand
the quiet authority with which he spoke of the contents of the Bible to others, independent of the views of
clergy or laymen, but never spoken as if of himself.
Bible study was the underlying factor of all his student work, and it was also to be the heart of all his
church activities. This work gradually took a definite
course, as the plan for uniting the believers within
the congregations in "inner circles" or "congregational
associations" engrossed his interest more and more.
This idea, which originated with Baron K. A. Wrede,
had been enthusiastically received by many pastors of
the land. It was hoped that the live Christians scattered throughout a congregation might, by fellowship
with each other, have their faith strengthened and
grow in holiness, and at the same time become the
salt which should gradually permeate the whole congregation. Such an idea would naturally appeal to
Baron Nicolay. He took an active interest in the work
of his friend in Helsingfors, and when in 1905 the
latter wrote that he was planning to come to Wiborg
to organise a congregational association there also, he
was very enthusiastic about the plan. To obtain a "chain

of people praying for the work" seemed to him to be the best preparation possible. "May God make plain your way before you. There must always be obstacles if there is to be blessing. Clouds are necessary for the rain to fall," he writes in this connection. And concerning the form of the work itself he adds: "If only there might be different groups according to the needs, and the Bible groups not meet in the churches, nor the pastors hold a monopoly on what is said." That he himself should be called to participate on a large scale in this work had not yet occurred to Baron Nicolay.

Baron Wrede visited Wiborg, and at a meeting on April 21st it was decided to organise a congregational association. Several Bible groups, including one for young women and one for older Christians, were to be formed, and joint monthly meetings held. But it soon became evident that the carrying out of the idea was not as easy as had been thought. To find leaders for the many groups seemed almost impossible; the pastors of the city who were interested in the cause were in need of help, and so it naturally followed that Baron Nicolay, during the months he spent at Monrepos, was drawn more closely into the work at Wiborg. He would either conduct a Bible class or introduce a discussion, and his advice was often sought on many different matters. But it was not until conditions in Russia relieved him of his duties in Petrograd that he could devote himself in earnest to the "Wiborg Congregational Association," of which he became the soul during the so-called "Red period," and the year following. Then did he begin to visit also other cities—Borgå, Ekenäs, Kotka—to propagate the idea which the association represented, and to organise new Bible groups. He became greatly attached to this work which brought him into touch with earnest Christians throughout the whole country. And the local pastors he usually found sympathetic and willing to support his endeavours.

Thus Paul Nicolay, towards the end of his life, was again led into a new path, the religious individualist was brought into a sphere of work in which he went hand in hand with the servants of the State Church. But this did not imply that he had lost any of his religious independence. In this work also he remained himself, a man with nothing of the official about him, and to whom ecclesiastical forms could never become an object in themselves, but merely one working means of leading souls to Jesus Christ. And, as has already been said, it was just in this that his contribution to the church lay. How this contribution was valued in the church itself is shown by the quaint Finnish name of honour bestowed on him with great affection at the conference at Leppakoski in 1918—"Pappien Paimen," the "Shepherd of the Pastors."

Another valuable contribution to the religious life was Paul Nicolay's introduction of regular "meetings for the deepening of spiritual life," patterned after the annual conferences at Keswick and Södertälje. It was primarily on his initiative that the first gathering of this kind met at Borgå in 1913. Here earnest Christians of different denominations met to seek together to enter deeper into the secrets of God's Kingdom, and receive more of His grace. Baron Nicolay hoped that much would come out of these conferences which would help to raise the Christian ideal and develop the spiritual life. The second "Keswick meeting" was held in September, 1919, also in Borgå. Paul Nicolay had lovingly prepared for it, but he was not to be permitted to attend it. During the days of the conference he lay on a bed of illness, and soon to him came the call to a more important and decisive meeting—the only one which no person can ever evade.

CHAPTER VIII

At Home and Among Friends

ON March 5, 1910, Paul Nicolay lost his mother. His relation to her had, up to the end, been the same as in his younger days; he had always shown her deep affection and respect, and she from her side had supported him in all his work and difficulties with her advice and intercession. His strivings she had always fully understood and sympathised with, in spite of some minor differences of opinion between mother and son concerning certain phases of the Christian life. He writes of her departure in a letter to Dr. Mott: [1]

"We have seen His good hand during her long wearisome illness, sparing her the awful sufferings which the doctors expected, sustaining her patience and faith during the times of great weakness, and giving her a peaceful end without pain. There is no doubt that it was a form of cancer, hopeless from the beginning, but without any palpable wounds or swellings. At first, in December, it seemed as if she were hastening towards a near and most painful end, but homeopathy brought relief. The feeling did not get better, however, and gradually she grew weaker and weaker until she passed away in slumber. A few days before her end she said: 'How delightful it would be to fall asleep on earth and awake in glory.' The last words

[1] Quoted from the original English letter.

I heard from her lips, the day before her departure, were: 'God bless you.' . . . We feel very peaceful, fully persuaded that it is God's doing, and that He does all things well and for the best. Last Wednesday we buried our Mother on our burial-island near Wiborg in Finland."

Paul Nicolay had a strong presentiment that the separation from his mother would not be for long, and he often felt after her death a sense of her nearness. In spite of the quiet assurance that "this was the work of God," the event affected him deeply. But yet it did not hinder him on the day after her death, from giving an address to Russian students, though he did so "with aching head and empty brain." The address was not powerful, but the rumour of the speaker's loss spread among the students, and his self-mastery impressed them more deeply than the most brilliant eloquence. The work must always take the foremost place in his life. "What I now most desire is to seek God's glory and interest above all else and fulfil the work which He has given me to do," he writes in September of the same year to a Finnish friend. "I believe that the greatness and depth of Christ's life is due to the *one* great purpose for which he lived—'I have glorified Thee on earth; I have finished the work which Thou gavest me to do' (John 17: 4). If only this were so in our lives! How zealous we would then be in spreading God's Kingdom, and how differently we would look on all failures, hardships, temptations, and suffering. . . . But how infinitely far from there I feel myself to be. This would be a life with *one pur-*

pose, one road, and one heart. May the Lord educate us to it."

When Paul Nicolay's life is viewed in its entirety, one realises that he had advanced pretty far in God's school along the line discussed above. His interest had gradually become centred around one great purpose, his strength implicitly consecrated to the work required by this purpose, so that it is hard to distinguish the boundary between his private life and his public work. His family must have accustomed themselves early to their only half possessing him. After his mother's death he continued to make his home with his two older sisters—the youngest had left home in 1890 to marry Count Konstantin von der Pahlen, a landowner from Courland—and he was devoted to them and conscious of their sympathetic solicitude for him and their interest in all his projects. But he who gives himself unreservedly to a great cause must to a certain extent become isolated even from his nearest and dearest. And this was also Paul Nicolay's experience. In St. Petersburg, as at Monrepos, he remained primarily the man in the ranks, who was not his own master and might never for a moment forget to obey higher commands.

Paul Nicolay had received in life much of what is considered to constitute happiness—social position, wealth, home conditions, all of which seemed calculated to make easy the way for him. But personal happiness was never permitted to become the aim of his strivings. What he possessed of temporal goods he regarded as a talent entrusted to him, and to his conscientious nature the responsibility of it seemed often heavy. To his many dependents and servants he regarded himself to be in material as well as spiritual debt, and his wealth he felt was for him to administer and not to use for his own pleasure. When, towards the close of his life his economic position was impaired by the Revolution, he considered selling the suburbs of Wiborg which belonged to Monrepos. But two questions concerned him most: how to arrange the sale so that his tenants should not suffer, and how to use aright the large means which would thus be his. For himself he was extremely economical, as we have seen in the case of his yacht.

In early years Baron Nicolay, guided by his Bible (especially Deut. 14:22), set aside a tenth of his income for religious and charitable objects. But this sum soon proved to be inadequate. In the first place his own work—his travels and the Russian Student Movement to which he gave substantial financial aid [1] —required considerable expenditures. Liberally also did he support foreign Missionary work for which he harboured a deep interest, and especially for the "China Inland Mission," with whose work he had become familiar through his English friends. Like many another wealthy person he received many visits and letters telling him of real or pretended need. As a rule he felt that he had no right to leave a request of this kind unnoticed, and usually tried to verify conditions described, turning to trusted friends for enlightenment

[1] Also the Finnish Student Christian Movement received financial aid from Baron Nicolay, although on a smaller scale. At his death this Movement received 30,000 Fmk willed to it. The Salvation Army's work in the slums of Wiborg had also a staunch friend in him.

or advice when unable to unravel them himself. If the needy person lived in Helsingfors he would direct his inquiries to K. A. Wrede, who, through his connections with the City Mission, could often assist him in his investigations. It pained him to see how often people tried to impose on him, and he was especially agitated by the number who came to him pretending to be Christians in the hope that that would further their cause. When there was real need, Baron Nicolay seldom showed any unwillingness to help. Thus the circle of his private charity was widened until, as far as his friends could see, a very large part of his income went in one way or another to helping needy people or beneficial enterprises.

It is hard for any one to say how widespread this charity really was; for Paul Nicolay followed literally the admonition in Christ's Sermon on the Mount, to give alms so that the left hand should not know what the right was doing. The help he gave was not in the form of startling donations written up in the papers or praised in brilliant speeches. Paul Nicolay was certainly not among those who receive all their reward on earth. Pastor H. Valkama, who as pastor in the suburbs of Wiborg had learned to know the owner of Monrepos, writes: "He said comparatively little about love, but he acted much more in the spirit of love. For innumerable are the distinctly material contributions through which he quietly brought joy and sunshine to needy abodes. He made no list of these his charitable deeds, nor did he permit any one to do so. But the Father of all orphans and Protector of widows remembers them still."

BARONESS SOPHIE NICOLAY
(The Mother of Paul Nicolay)

Naturally a very large part of Baron Nicolay's attention concerned his dependents in the suburbs of Wiborg—Pikiruukki, Saunalahti, Likolampi, and Sorvali. As far as his time permitted he was a good landlord to them. He was conscientious, serious, and incorruptibly just in his relation to the leaseholders of his land and to his workmen. Always ready to help where help was needed, he required from all in return precision in their work. The honesty and punctuality which were his he sought to instil in those around him. Thus he, who was usually amiable, might be severe with any leaseholder who, without informing him in advance, neglected to pay his rent at the appointed time. If any were unable to pay promptly he *expected* to be notified of it, and when that happened he considered the matter settled for the time being. It was carelessness and indifference which aroused his deep displeasure. Even the servants of the house recognised the Baron's requirements of punctuality, which they often found hard to meet. But many a time they have stood blushing with embarrassment before their master while he, sterner far with himself than with others, in his courteous way apologised for some trivial neglect of which *he* felt himself guilty. "How often had I not been more careless myself!" said a servant maid in speaking of the Baron after his death. As another characteristic especially marked in him she mentioned his *patience,* that "jewel" which he himself had possibly regarded as the most difficult for him to acquire.

Thus Baron Nicolay accomplished much good at Monrepos, not merely through what he did, but also through what he was. Eagerly did he observe the spiritual growth of his dependents. When in his later years he visited the estate, he attended every Sunday morning the modest little chapel of Hiekka. "He came there in prayer," writes Pastor Valkama, "listened prayerfully to the words of the preacher, and prayed for him." And in this way he was brought into intimate fellowship with the pastor as well as the congregation, and soon on his own initiative began an organised work to gather the young people in Hiekka for prayer and Bible study. This work is still being carried on both in Hiekka and Likolampi, and its extension into the other suburbs has also been planned. When the question of building a meeting house in Sorvali was brought up, Baron Nicolay was enthusiastic about the idea, donated the ground for the building, and followed with interest the further development of the enterprise.

Long before this time Baron Nicolay had started the daily custom of assembling the Finnish speaking inhabitants of Monrepos at half past eight every morning for prayer. He would read a portion from the New Testament, and himself lead the singing with his unmusical but fairly true voice. In the nineties he had also begun to conduct morning prayers for the Russian speaking servants of the house. His Mother, and later his sisters, assembled for prayers all, both guests and servants, who understood German. Thus the entire household was gradually permeated by the spirit of its owner.

It is evident that the months spent each year at Monrepos were far from being a time of complete rest

for Baron Nicolay.   These visits to his ancestral home
were also trying on account of the unsuitability of the
climate, owing to its low situation near a bay, Suom-
envedenpohja, from which damp mists rose morning
and evening.   Naturally this was not wholesome to
one who, like Baron Nicolay, suffered from malaria.
In the autumn of 1910 he writes:[1] "I get along as
well as I can here at Monrepos.   There is something
in the water and air that has an injurious effect on
me, and I am often dissatisfied with it and with myself.   I think at times that it is God's will that I should
not be rooted to this spot lest I should leave the student work in Russia."   This thought, that there might
be a special significance in the discomfort experienced
at Monrepos, had already occurred to him when in
1908 he asks himself: "Why should I not have a home
where I could live?"   He adds, "If it is for student
work I am to suffer, then student work must be worth
it."

Thus Baron Nicolay's fondness for the place which
his forefathers had loved, and where he himself had
spent so many happy hours in his youth, diminished
with the years.   In the beautifying of the parks he
took no interest, and was content to preserve its already existing constructions, which was burdensome
enough in itself.   The park that was open to the public became a source of sorrow on account of the van-
dalism perpetrated by some of the promenaders.
Benches were overturned or moved from their places,
the walls of the pavilions covered with inscriptions,
and monuments injured—even the crosses on the

[1] Quoted from his English diary.

graves at Ludwigstein had more than once been mo-
lested. Therefore Baron Nicolay, who longed to believe in the good in human nature, was depressed at
Monrepos by being forced into painful contact with
the bad and unsightly side of human nature.

It can hardly, therefore, be wondered at if at Monrepos he felt more tired, less able to resist his own
weakness, less "in his element" than in many other
places. Here also did he manfully strive to fulfil his
duty, but the battle was often hard, and the remark
of a friend that he did not have any joyful feeling of
being at home was perhaps not altogether unwarranted.
The cheerfulness which was one of his greatest charms
was often completely lacking when on his estate. In
the company of both his sisters he spent many a happy
and peaceful hour, but when of an autumn he would
visit the old house alone he was especially overpowered by its inherent sadness. In moments spent alone
in the little upstairs room, which the master of Monrepos had chosen to be his own and where the simple
cross above the bed was one of the few adornments,
there could arise in his heart a burning longing for
those treasures of this world which had not been
granted him to possess—a loving wife and happy children. Thus in the autumn of 1913 he writes:[1] "All
these days I have such a gnawing pain of loneliness, regret that I did not marry when I was young. It seems
so unnatural not to have one's own home. But it is too
late for regrets. If I had married, I should never
have had the interest and perseverance and means to
work for the Student Movement. Maybe there is re-

[1] Quoted from his English diary.

ward in the next world, but why a reward when there is no merit? Maybe this gnawing pain of loneliness is to hurry me to St. Petersburg and stimulate me for the work. The vine is pruned to make it concentrate its vital sap in one direction. It looks as if God had pruned me, cutting off other prospects, to make me go in one direction. Maybe one must bear a wound in one's breast to drop sap and be sensitive and fruitful. . . . Christ says: 'Whosoever loses home . . . or wife . . . for my sake. . . .'[1] Anyhow, my loss has been the means of helping some others morally and spiritually, and that is some consolation."

It was the thought of the Student Movement that helped him through these dark hours, his oft recurring consciousness that he must bleed in order to bless. So now, as in 1899, he restrained himself from these dark thoughts. Although he would at times speak of himself as a misanthrope, he never let bitterness be rooted in his heart. He who led a solitary life was brought by his relation to God into an exceptionally warm fellowship with many around him. Paul Nicolay was able to give much, and he also received much in return. It is impossible to speak of him without at least mentioning the friends in whose affection and whose hospitable homes he found a compensation for what he himself was deprived of, something of the sunshine which had not fallen across his own path. With a noble nature's capacity for sympathy, he could enjoy to the full the happiness of his friends, and never was

---

[1] Of significance is a note in Baron Nicolay's Bible at the conclusion to Matt. 19:29. "God's servant will surely be more than compensated for what he loses, but do not think about it. Don't bargain with God."

his face so illumined as when visiting them in their homes.

Among these, Mr. Wilder's home in Norway occupies one of the foremost places. In the beautiful villa "Norheim" at Veldre, near Lake Mjösen, Baron Nicolay felt wonderfully at home. Every one, who wandered up the woodland trail which leads from Veldre station through dark pine-clad heights up to the white house surrounded by leafy silver birches and the garden bright with flowers,[1] has experienced the feeling of home and peace which meets one even on arrival, and realises how this place could offer rest and happiness to all who visited here. It was not the beauty of nature and the lovely view over the lake alone, nor the clear mild air, but the warmth of the reception by host and hostess, and above all the feeling that this home was "built upon a rock" which brought a beneficial balm to the soul. The home was open to the people of the countryside and to their children, and it also became a natural place of meeting for all foreign Christian workers who passed through Norway. Around the cause of God's Kingdom it centred. "Work, study, play, being out in beauteous nature, all is done in the happy, quiet spirit which knows that God is the first and the last." This was an ideal atmosphere for Paul Nicolay. But of greater value than all else was the fellowship with Mr. Wilder himself, whose happy, harmonious temperament seemed to supplement his own which was more marked by struggle, and there existed between these two men a deep

[1] From "Ad Lucem." November 5, 1910—"A Visit in Mr. Wilder's Home."

and spiritual friendship. "We seemed to know each other and understand each other fully," wrote Mr. Wilder after his friend's departure. "The seasons spent together in Norway meant more to me than words can express—those long walks under the pines, in which we shared each other's experiences and spoke of the deep things of life and what Christ meant to us."

But if the older members of the family at Veldre were happy in their fellowship with Baron Nicolay, no less was his society appreciated by the youngest in the home. He was very fond of children, and the four little girls at Norheim could always count on him for a lively playmate. After a serious Bible study he would go with them to finish a paper kite, or organise a battle with the beloved fir cones as weapons, and great was the children's delight. At meals he could with true boyish recklessness strew sugar on the eggs or pepper on a dish which was meant to be without this condiment, and in the evenings he had perchance a surprise in store—fireworks, which were exultantly hailed by all. Is it strange that the children knew how to appreciate their dear "Pluncle," as they called Baron Nicolay—a name formed by the combination of his Christian name and the English "uncle"?

In Finland also did Paul Nicolay have friends in whose company he felt entirely at home. The names of both Barons Henrik and Karl August Wrede have already often been mentioned, and we have seen what it meant to Baron Nicolay to be associated with the latter in his work. They had met in 1894 at a time when Baron K. A. Wrede had not yet decided for

Christ, and Nicolay's life and words were a great help to him, not only at that time but during his whole life of service for Christ. Similarly Baron Wrede's friendship was also of great help to Paul Nicolay. They often met, and became comrades in their work, in the most beautiful sense of the word, at the Finnish Student Conferences and later in the field of church work. Just because their development was at first in somewhat different directions, though their purpose was always the same, the outcome of their fellowship was still richer. The days Baron Nicolay spent with K. A. Wrede, in Haga near Helsingfors in the winter and in the summer at Karlstorp near Wredeby, he always looked back on with joy; and in times of long separation a generous exchange of letters kept him in touch with his friend and his family, "Paulus" and his "dear Titus" as the letters usually read.

There was yet another spot in Finland where Baron Nicolay was the most cherished of friends, and where he always loved to visit because of the unfeigned and unlimited sympathy and understanding which he found there. This spot was Toivola, the home of Baron Henrik Wrede and his "God-sent," as he at times called the Baroness Ellen Wrede. Here, as at Norheim, he need not subject himself to any restraint, and, as there, he could inhale at Toivola pure rest-giving country air and bask in the sunshine of family happiness and friendliness. After a stay at a health resort abroad or in Finland, he liked to come for an "after cure" to Toivola. Many anecdotes which his friends can tell reveal the feeling of being at home which was his when here; how in the evenings he demanded the right to prepare and serve tea, an accomplishment which he had acquired in Russia and England, often going to the kitchen himself to fetch the tea water; how at every visit he would accompany his host to the garden or chicken coop to share his joy in every new or old sight. He did this more usually from sympathy with his friend's enterprises, for he himself had little interest in country establishments. The only animals he really knew anything about were dogs, of which Monrepos has always had a large supply, while Toivola made a specialty of fine varieties of horses, cattle, and poultry. He would often amuse himself watching ducklings and goslings splashing in the river, but the details concerning the different breeds of birds and cattle did not interest him. Neither was he familiar with plant life, and had often occasion to be ashamed of his superficial knowledge of Botany. There were other phenomena of nature that interested him, and he loved on a clear autumn evening to study the stars, with which he was very familiar. When Baron Wrede reproached him for his lack of interest in agriculture, he sought on his side to arouse his friend's enthusiasm for the marvellous discoveries in the field of science, which he had always eagerly followed.

At Toivola he had also a friend in the young daughter of the house, whom he gladly helped with her schoolwork, not only in language study but also with her assignments in Geography, Physics, and Mathematics. Several hours a day did Baron Nicolay devote here to his work, but he found time to enjoy the out-of-doors as well. Trips on skis in winter, and in summer quiet hours by the river with a fishing rod or walks in the lovely pine woods were refreshing, and he treasured them still more highly as they were of necessity a rare occurrence.

But not as the entertaining and friendly man of the world do his friends at Toivola like to recall him, but as the quiet, earnest "man of God" who by his prayer, his conversation and his whole personality opened up to them new vistas in the world of the Spirit. Such also is the memory left by him in the many homes abroad and in Finland which he visited during his missionary journeys. This memory is preserved as a precious treasure by many more friends than a biography can mention. And to him did the loving reception he met with everywhere become part of the reward which the Lord, with whom he never bargained, with generous hand bestowed upon His servant.

CHAPTER IX

The Time of Departure

"For to me to live is Christ and to die is gain." [1]

IN January, 1917, Baron Nicolay lay severely ill at Monrepos. During his illness his thoughts were continually centred around the work in Russia which he had not yet been forced to give up.[2] "Who will fill my place for the students if I am called away?" he writes in his diary. "If I die as I am now, it would mean that God could not attain more with me in this life. It would be a rather sad end of an at first seemingly promising life. . . . It is a solemn thought to me to be near my end, maybe, and still such a bad and poor Christian." And when his health was slightly improved he prayed that God "might let him keep that sensitive, receptive heart" which had been his during the days of his illness.

His health remained poor for some time, and as before he was afraid of tuberculosis; but the examination revealed nothing of the kind. He felt very tired, and the notes in his diary show that he had not abandoned all thoughts of death. On his birthday, July 14th, he writes:[2] "If it is God's will I would gladly leave this earth and go to Him. I would also gladly live on if

[1] These words from Phil. 1 are intended to form the inscription on the monument to be raised on Paul Nicolay's grave.
[2] Quoted from his English diary.

only I can work with full power and not half speed like this last year." This was perhaps an unconscious echo of Paul's words in the first chapter of Philippians (v. 22). And as to the great apostle when he wrote these words to the Church at Philippi, so also to Paul Nicolay did the foreboding of a fast approaching departure become linked to the thought of meeting the Lord he served. "If Christ should come to-morrow it would be my only consolation to know that I belong to Him," he wrote in September. The conception of Christ's second coming which might possibly be in the near future, perhaps in his own lifetime, had become more and more a reality to him.

When this conception—in the year 1910—first became precious to him, he had no desire to make it the object of public discussion and interpretation. "I believe like you that it is better not to say too much about the Lord's return, but to be prepared for it myself," he wrote in 1915 to K. A. Wrede. "But when we meet an earnest Christian it is our duty to help him to get light on this matter, so as to await that day with a joyful earnestness, without fear or trembling." The development of the war, the great political upheavals, the ferment of all minds, the shameful triumph of evil in all spheres, strengthened him still more in the belief that Christ Himself must interfere in this world tragedy, that the promise of His return to save His people was now about to be fulfilled.

Baron Nicolay came into close touch with the terrors of the time. Thus, he once found himself by chance beside the bloody corpse of his murdered cousin, General Stackelberg, on the streets in Petrograd, and was immediately subject to arrest by the soldiers. It was not fear of personal suffering that drove him to seek comfort in a superhuman hope:[1] "The peace of God continues to surround us," he wrote in March, while the roar of cannon filled the city. But he was greatly pained by seeing the power of sin in the lives of men. With a "joyful earnestness" during the last years of his life he therefore awaited the great event. And when from reading a study on the book of Revelation the thought had come to him that it should be on the day of the Jewish New Year Feast, he would yearly at this time write his closest friends: "Do you remember that the 'critical day' will soon be here again?"

There was nothing restless or fantastical about this expectation, but rather something of the childish Christmas spirit which cast a cheerful, hallowed glow over the sorrowful and work-filled week-day. And gradually it came to be a vital matter to him to lead others also into the way of waiting and watching. We read in a letter to Mr. Wood, May 1917, a part of which has already been quoted:[2]

"This most terrible war seems to be drawing to a close on account of prostration of all parties and lack of food. Some signs seem to indicate the approaching coming of our Lord, the immense growth of social democracy and anarchy of an extreme anti-Christian kind, and on the other hand, in this country (Russia) many hearts thirsting for the Gospel and free ac-

---

[1] Quoted from his English diary.
[2] Quoted from the original English.

cess everywhere. Do you know that the whole Mohammedan World is expecting the coming of Jesus Christ who, they say, 'did not die on the cross but was taken up to heaven and will return to reign on earth as a Moslem prince, will kill the antichrist, and will die and be buried in Medina next to Mohammed'? And do you know that the Buddhist world expects a reincarnation of Buddha under the name of Metteya (Messiah) who is to be the personification of love? Pity the Christians seem not to reckon with this coming event, at least not the church at large."

It was as if a quiet concentration of power, a preparation for the storms of the coming year, was now taking place in Paul Nicolay's soul. Many who met him at Runni, where he went for his health in 1917, received an ineffaceable impression of him. Little did he know when he returned to Monrepos that his ancestral estate was to become his only home until the time of his death. He had profited by his stay at Runni, but the needed rest after it he found as hard to obtain that autumn as did any one else. The restlessness of the time burst irresistibly over the old estate with its peaceful traditions. Even during the summer all imperial busts and statues had had to be removed from the park, as one of them had been smashed to pieces. But, before long, events far more dreadful were to take place in the close vicinity of Monrepos. September 11th, a Russian artillery captain was hung by the soldiers in the wood outside the park, and not long after, twenty-seven other officers shared this terrible fate. Even to Baron Nicolay's home did soldiers come "in search of officers," and once actually for the purpose of arresting him himself, but on this occasion one of the Russian workmen on the estate succeeded in averting the danger from his master.

During the November strike [1] Baron Nicolay was very active, speaking at the request of the "Congregational Association" at Wiborg several times to smaller groups as well as to a larger audience. He now also began to hold a series of Bible studies on the Epistle to the Philippians, that epistle of suffering and victorious joy which had absorbed him so long, and to which he had written a commentary for the Russian students similar to his "hand-book" on the Gospel of Mark. In the worst of the "November days" discontinuing the meetings had been seriously considered, but decided against. Many an evening did Baron Nicolay walk alone through the dark woods of evil repute on his way to and from the city, and he rejoiced that God kept him throughout from fear.

"We are attending God's school, and learning to have faith without sight," he wrote K. A. Wrede, when the strike was at last over. "It is a precious lesson to learn that we can in times of real danger or need actually rest in peace, because God takes care of His children. We are continually being reminded that the presence, protection and faithfulness of the Lord are a reality."

Paul Nicolay now felt more than ever before that he must "be the mouth of the Lord and proclaim His message." In Wiborg he not only conducted Bible stud-

[1] A universal labour strike in connection with the Bolsheviks in Petrograd, when the Reds in many places first took the power into their hands.

ies, but gave lectures and introduced a discussion on "What demands does this time make on a Christian?" At the beginning of December he spoke in the Russian Institute of Science in the city on the World's Student Christian Federation, and towards the close of the month visited Petrograd where he gave an address on John the Baptist. Although he enjoyed being far from the throngs of this great city, he hoped that the stay at Monrepos might be only a temporary respite and that "the Lord next year should again want to make use of His weak servant." On January 24, 1918, he again went to Petrograd, this time to speak in the city condemned to unheard-of sufferings on Revelation 21 : 5—"Behold I make all things new"—his last message of hope to the people among whom he had laboured so long.

On New Year's Eve Baron Nicolay had written: [1] "So ends this dreadful year, the worst any of us has seen, and yet a year during which God's goodness and faithfulness have never failed us." The new year was to become even worse than the preceding one, but the same peace enveloped him, and God used his servant unceasingly. As all the ways leading out were gradually closed, Baron Nicolay devoted himself more to the work of Wiborg's "Congregational Association." He concluded his Bible studies on the Philippians at the regular Thursday meetings, and began a series of studies on the parables of Jesus—Luke 15, the wedding feast, the sower, the husbandman and the vineyard, the ten virgins, the ten pounds—which continued until May, through the entire "Period of the

[1] Quoted from his English diary.

LUDWIGSTEIN, BARON NICOLAY'S PLACE OF BURIAL

THE GRAVE

Red Terror" which in Wiborg began in the end of
January and lasted to the closing days of April. Of
his experiences at this time Baron Nicolay wrote on
February 13th to Dr. Mott: [1]

"We are living in awful times, as you well know,
both in Russia and also here in Finland where we have
civil war. The south, including Åbo, Helsingfors,
Tammerfors, Kotka, and Wiborg, are in the hands
of the Red guards, twin brothers of the Russian Bolsheviks, who are introducing here the same monstrous
socialistic theories as there. . . . To the eye of faith
this is a necessary judgment of God which will not
continue forever. Human life is very cheap now, both
in Russia and in Finland. It is very unpleasant to feel
yourself a captive of a revolutionary mob and its
theoretical leaders, and to know that actual famine is
threatening you even now; and yet it is a school of
faith. We have as yet suffered no want and have been
protected in a very providential way. God will, we
trust, remove this scourge very quickly, as soon as His
time will be ripe. God is ploughing Russia and Finland; that is a sure sign that He intends to sow."

As is apparent in the letter, Baron Nicolay did not
have to suffer personally at the hands of the "Reds."
To be sure the Red guards had an investigation made
of the house at Monrepos by a man who was born on
the estate, but they behaved properly and even seemed
embarrassed, perhaps because the guide who was
friendly towards the owner of the place was loath to
make the investigation. Baron Nicolay was allowed

[1] Quoted from the original English letter.

to continue his religious work unhindered, and he considered this a great privilege. He was glad to be able to concentrate on *one* form of work, and later he wrote that from a physical point of view this had been been the quietest winter he had ever known, for he had no need to travel nor divide his strength.

He was happy to see how the need brought many souls nearer to God. "During the fire of the Revolution," he later wrote, "the hearts of men were uneasy and the churches were filled as never before. I was forced many a time to preach from the pulpit; and although I did not then relish it, I now recall with gratitude the time with Pastor N., when we together served men in their need." The work he referred to consisted of a series of addresses delivered in the church, half apologetic in character—as the talk on "Two cogent reasons for belief in Christ"—and in part purely edifying—as "Christ in the storm." These addresses were attended by many who had never been regular churchgoers nor eager to attend Bible classes and congregational evening meetings; and something of the *reality* of God faced them in the quiet faith of the speaker and his absolute certainty of the "things which are not seen."

But Baron Nicolay did not neglect the Russians who were driven by the storms of the time to Wiborg. Among them was the wife of Colonel Paschkov who had settled in a villa, near the city, where the fugitives would gather for prayer and meetings, which were often led by Baron Nicolay. Thus was established a religious union which lasted even after his death and the departure of Madame Paschkov.

The universally abnormal conditions began to seem more and more oppressive as Spring approached. In April came the great reaction, bringing relief but also in its wake new suffering and new sorrow. On the 24th the "White Guards" laid siege to Wiborg, and on the following day came crowds of fugitives, mostly poor women and children, from the surrounding districts to seek shelter at Monrepos. Here for several days they were cared for, and under the severest cannonading, when shells exploded close to the building, Baron Nicolay read to his agitated guests the forty-sixth Psalm—"God is our refuge and strength." As far as Monrepos was concerned the words of the Psalm were literally fulfilled, for not even a windowpane was broken during the bombardment.

On the morning of the 29th, Baron Nicolay was summoned, and saw to his amazement a company of young men in grey uniforms, the White Guard of the Kajana regiment. Wiborg was captured and the great tension was over; but the ensuing days were very hard for Baron Nicolay. News of murders in Wiborg and other cities now began to reach him, and he heard about many victims of the battle. He was greatly moved to learn of the death of both of the brothers Bruun, sons of an old friend of his. As soon as possible he went to see Baron Henrik Wrede in his home, and rejoiced to find him safe in spite of his nearness to the sorely afflicted Kouvala. But there were many gruesome deeds of which he learned here.

That all unrighteousness had not been overcome by the victory of the "Whites," Paul Nicolay with his clear insight into true values could not fail to see.

Even in the first days after the capture of Wiborg he witnessed some terrible scenes, as when on his way from Monrepos to the city he saw how the victors cut down a number of Russians, among whom were many innocent ones, who waved their handkerchiefs in despair as they implored mercy. The sight of prisoners being hurried to the barracks made him think seriously. He was in his whole nature and point of view essentially a people's man, and the Christian was stronger in him than the aristocrat; and although he realised that justice must have its way, it grieved him to see how *vengeance* had a free hand at a time like this. He therefore, along with the Chancellor of Commerce, William Hackman, had published on April 30th in the Wiborg newspaper the following appeal to those in power:

"At this solemn hour when much is at stake, may voices be raised in a plea for passionless measures and wise discernment in punishment towards those of the children of our land who are guilty.

"That society must be freed from unscrupulous perpetrators of violence is a sad necessity. But the greater part of the workers now imprisoned are not among them. Many of our workers belonged to the Red guard, being forced to join because they had formerly belonged to the Labour Union. They had been led astray by agitators, and now they have repented deeply and are embittered against their leaders.

"Would that our liberators and we ourselves might treat this class with wise forbearance and humanity! If

these labourers be blindly punished their embitterment
will be great and the wound within our society aggra-
vated; but if they be treated with wise forbearance and humanity, one step will be gained towards
the restoration of inner peace, the diminishing of class
hatred, and the rebuilding of society.

"May vengeance and hatred not darken the dawn
of our young and independent government."

In his personal relation to his dependents Baron
Nicolay, says Pastor Valkama, never allowed himself
to be influenced by their political views, when it was a
case of giving them the material help they needed.
The order issued by the authorities for all Russians to
leave the country within ten days seemed to him a
bit of "madness." Among his six hundred and four-
teen leaseholders one hundred and fifteen were Russians, whose pitiable plight aroused his deep sympathy,
so that he decided to await the Commandant in order
to plead their cause before him.

But in spite of all this Baron Nicolay did not give
up his religious work. He felt that he dared not do
this. "Rast' ich, so rost' ich," is engraved on an ancient German sword, we read in his diary. During the
summer he read proof for the Swedish translation of
his Bible study on Philippians which was now to be
printed. After concluding his talks on the Parables
of Jesus, May 16th, he had undertaken new tasks, was
studying the Epistle of James, and delivered at the
deaconess' home a series of expositions on the Prophet
Elijah.

In August he was invited to attend the conference

in Södertälje, and wrote to Mr. Sloan: "I am already looking forward to the Södertälje conference in Sweden, to which Prince Bernadotte and Dr. Fries so kindly invited me. To bring together and help strengthen the spiritual life of 'God's scattered children' is something for which Christ died. I feel that we ought to have more of this kind of work. We often hold evangelistic meetings within and outside the church, but we ought to organise a series of four or five meetings for the deepening of the spiritual life of God's people. Nothing of this kind has as yet really been started. The holding of conferences should be one progressive step in this direction. For the present this is almost, if not entirely, impossible on account of the difficulty of securing food for a large number of people. . . . Everything is being turned upside down in this world, and the return of our Lord Jesus seems more and more to become the solution toward which all the confusion is moving. It does not look as if this terrible war, which has been called a suicide of Europe, will soon come to an end. We ought better to understand the possibility that the time of the heathen is drawing to an end."

In the same letter Baron Nicolay informs Mr. Sloan about his friends in Russia, and continues: "It is terrible to live in a land of anarchy. You learn to understand in a very real way our Lord's words in Matt. 24: 12—'Because iniquity shall abound, the love of many shall wax cold.' "

That the war, "the suicide of Europe," became to Paul Nicolay, as to all thinking men, the typification of all evil, need hardly be mentioned. But he realised, as has already been shown, that the war could become an instrument in the hand of God, a means of accomplishing His great purpose for humanity. Individualist as he was, he would not take a definite stand with reference to the question of war; that was a matter he felt that every one should decide for himself according to God's special guidance. Thus a pacifist he was not; for he saw in the Sermon on the Mount a standard for the private life of a Christian.

Baron Nicolay hoped greatly for intervention by the Allies against the Bolsheviks. He did not live to see the uselessness of material arms against them, nor the definite degeneracy of the "peace." But he realised even now, that God knew best how long Russia must be ploughed before "His seed would be driven deep enough down," and that "His time" could not be hastened by artificial means.

In November in a letter to Mr. Sloan Baron Nicolay gives an account of his impressions of the Conference at Södertälje, which was held that month. He speaks of the great joy of fellowship with other Christians, among whom Dr. and Mrs. Fries were mentioned, and says "it was such a treat." Although he had a high opinion of some of the speakers, like Prince Bernadotte, he felt that the conference could not be compared with "what he had seen and heard at Keswick in former years." He mentions in conclusion the opportunities for work in Finland:[1]

"New doors are opening for me in Finland for religious activity. In the Swedish-speaking parishes we

[1] Quoted from the original English letter.

want to stir up spiritual life and form the would-be Christians into inner circles, which would meet together, and have Bible study groups, and keep warm. At present they are lost in the mass of nominal church members, and do not even know each other. The inner circle should be the soul of the congregation, a centre of life, warmth, and activity, even when the pastor is not what he ought to be. I have had the privilege of visiting a few places on this errand, and hope to start to-morrow for the town of Kotka for a week. If we could form such inner circles in a number of places it would be quite natural to have them meet at certain times for general conferences. The educated classes are very little reached in Finland, and dreadfully ignorant of spiritual things."

More than ever did Baron Nicolay ignore health and strength. He felt that he had a great deal to accomplish, and that the time was short. In a letter written in August to Baron Wrede he writes: "I have a feeling that we in Finland will not be allowed to fold our hands, but that we must be prepared to hear the 'message of Haggai.' May God grant us wisdom and help us find His plan for the Kingdom of God in Finland. One must recall our Lord's words in John 9: 14." [1]

In Sweden, at the conference in Södertälje and also in Stockholm where he broke the journey, he gave several addresses on themes, including two which he had especially on his heart: "A Better Life," and "The Re-

---

[1] "I must work the works of Him that sent me while it is day; the night cometh, when no man can work."

turn of Christ." On his return to Finland he devoted himself entirely, as the letter to Mr. Sloan suggests, to the task of building up inner circles in the congregations, visiting also several cities in the south to arouse interest in this, the cause he loved. And great was his joy whenever he met with appreciation of the deep significance of the organisation. When a pastor in Borgå used the expression "A Union of the Friends of the Lord," Baron Nicolay immediately voiced his appreciation of the name he had employed—"The Friends of the Lord—that is just the right term!" And in his diary we find the little episode noted down.

Towards the close of the year tiredness again began to steal over him; even in his addresses a certain exhaustion often being noticeable. He was conscious of it himself, and often troubled by it. At the end of a series of talks he wrote: "I feel as if I had been taking a lot of examinations." But he succeeded, nevertheless, through his fight against weariness and through his characteristic self-denial in giving his audience unusually much. For never before had he been more anxious to "die himself" in order to lead the cause of his Lord to victory. Once, after addressing a gathering in Kotka, he was thanked in the name of all present by one who said he had been like John Hus, lifting a lamp to the Gospel but himself remaining in the shadow. Of this he wrote in his diary, "This word rejoiced me more than any she could have said; it was just what I had prayed for before coming here."

December was spent by Baron Nicolay in the quiet of Monrepos, engrossed in the cares connected with

the sale of property in the suburbs and in the writing
down of a Bible study on the First Epistle to the Thessalonians, which he had given in Wiborg. He and his
sisters knelt in prayer while this year, the last he was
to live through in its entirety, came to a close. In the
usual New Year's meditation in his diary we read:[1]
"A terrible year—revolution, civil war, and famine;
and yet God has provided for us in every way most
graciously, and we have lacked nothing. I pray Him
to be with us this coming year and to make me a better
Christian."

A better Christian—these words might be said to be
the motto of the last year of Paul Nicolay's life. In
January he wrote:[1] "Am not at all feeling bright and
hopeful for the beginning of this year. Maybe it is
physical depression. Whatever is to happen, my main
duty is to keep trusting God quietly. Then all is all
right, and even violent death would be nothing to dis-
turb my peace." He continues his work in the churches
of various cities during the winter and spring, and also
keeps up his Bible studies in Wiborg. But throughout,
it was as if _one_ thought, the consciousness of all that
he still lacked in holiness was, along with his intense
desire for the return of Christ, gaining more and more
dominion over his inner life.[1] "God's aim with us is
not only to have us saved, but to 'slipa ädelstenar till
Kristi krona.' "[2] The suffering, caused by the physical weakness he had daily to overcome in his work, he
thought of merely as the instrument of the "grinder"
and was eager only to be complete victor over his old,

[1] Quoted from his English diary.
[2] Grind the jewels for the crown of Christ.

not yet entirely subdued, ego. His shattered nerves often tempted him to be hasty or impatient; but he did not retire from active life on account of this personal excuse. "During a temptation to unfriendliness the thought 'deny thyself' brought immediate relief," he once writes. And on another occasion it is, "Crucify thyself." "He can not be my disciple" in any other way. No comforting words can avail except this be one's attitude toward the ego.

In the spring Baron Nicolay's heart showed symptoms of weakness, and the doctor forbade his preaching in churches, which injunction he partly ignored. In the congregational groups his Bible studies were at this time on the Second Epistle to the Thessalonians and on the Book of Job. When he was to speak he experienced, as during the early years of his religious work, a deep dread, a feeling of impotence for the task. "The Devil can frighten but he can not hinder," words which Mr. Wilder had once said to him, and which he would often quote, were now as before made real to him. He always sought strength in quietness before God. At times he felt even too weak to pray, and he then tried to devote an hour to "quiet waiting on God." "It is hard, but it ought to help," he wrote of this. In May he held his last Bible study for the congregational groups, on receiving the Holy Spirit. In commenting on Romans 7:6 he emphasised that one condition for this was self-denial, another faith in the Holy Spirit. Both conditions were equally unchangeable. When some one later insisted that all one had to do was to wait for the Spirit, Baron Nicolay replied: "That is true, but *in order to wait we must be obedient.*"

This thought, that the Spirit can not grow within a man until his heart is as it should be, he also emphasised in his Bible courses at the Y. W. C. A. Summer School at Vasa in July, where he went straight from the Student Conference at Ilmajoki. At Vasa—contrary to all expectations, for he did not usually enjoy conferences just for women—he really experienced happy days. He felt that there was almost "revival in the air." And those who were then present at Vasa had a feeling that there radiated from Paul Nicolay a power which was not his own. In his usual quiet way he went around—possibly less inclined than ever before to assert himself—mingling naturally with the delegates, and with his same quiet sense of humour. But his face seemed to reveal something new.

"The beautiful meetings of the day were over," we read in an article by Madame af Forselles in "Ad Lucem." "The Northern bright spirit of night had settled over land and sea, and we were walking quietly homeward. The last rays of the sun cast a strange gleam over our path. I said something about how helpful the day's Bible Study had been, and how real to me had become God's power to save me from my own ego. 'What I said came straight from the furnace,' slowly answered Baron Nicolay. Was it the sun's last farewell which was reflected on his countenance, or was another light already enveloping him? I know not; but one thing I know, that the meaning of Jesus' words, 'Ye are the light of the world,' then became real to me, while I became suddenly aware that Paul Nicolay was not long to remain with us."

There were not many who, like Madame af Forselles, already surmised the imminent departure of Baron Nicolay. He had never been strong, and those who saw him in full activity at Ilmajoki and Vasa during the summer days, with his eyes fixed on new tasks, could not naturally realise that his working day was nearing its end. To him, as we know, the thought of death had never seemed very distant, and is often mentioned in letters and in his diary of his last summer.

In the beginning of June he wrote to Baron K. A. Wrede: "It seems monotonous and boresome here, especially since I can not walk fast or exert myself without getting out of breath. The doctors say that it is not heart failure but hardening of the arteries. They are all reminders of age and that we have not here a lasting abode, but look for and expect a better one." Yet immediately afterwards he looks forward once more to the long-planned-for Keswick Conference. "You will be sixty years old on September 18th, when we will all be together in Borgå. Henrik promises to be there. Remember this meeting daily in your prayers. For if God's Spirit is not there, all will be in vain." From Nådendal, "that boresome place" where he had been forced to go from Vasa for his health, and where he finds the hours spent alone on the rocks are the best, he writes to the same friend on July 13th:

"As I am about to enter on my sixtieth year tomorrow, I would like to end this year with a little talk with you. The doctor here says that I am suffering from advanced hardening of the arteries, and does not hope much from the baths here. This does not worry me, but stimulates me rather to live as close as possible to the Lord during the remainder of my life."

In Nådendal he felt that he had "far too little to do," and rejoices over every occasion to be of service, especially if he could help a seeking soul by a private conversation. One day he spoke in the chapel of the town. And during his whole stay he also kept up the extensive correspondence, which he had gradually come to regard as "a part of the service." This correspondence was now chiefly concerning the autumn conference at Borgå, to preparation, for which he devoted himself as far as possible after having left Nådendal with joy on August 7th. He felt, in spite of everything, strengthened by the cure.[1] "My nerves are much better, my memory has also grown a trifle better," he writes in his diary, "and that ought to be profitable for the work." He was at that time also working on his "Studies on the Second Epistle to the Thessalonians"— a book which was practically completed by August 19th.

Three days later Baron Nicolay was taken ill and had to send for the doctor, who diagnosed it as paratyphoid. His first thought was,[1] "As I am always unwell before important meetings, this may be an 'introduction' to Borgå meeting. If God wants to weaken me, I have no objection." He could at first simply not believe that he would have to stay away from this con-

[1] Quoted from his English diary.

ference, whose every detail he had lived himself into. During his illness he writes, September 8th, to his English friend Mr. Sloan about all his plans and fears for the Conference. He also writes of his work in the churches, and adds, "Perhaps I shall continue it this winter, if God does not lay me aside." *God makes no mistakes*—this comforting thought came to Paul Nicolay when he saw the day for the opening of the Borgå Conference approach without any improvement in his condition. When this day, the 16th, dawned, he wrote to his friend at Karlstorp: "I am still ill and in my fourth week in bed, but the fever is beginning to diminish. Not to have been able to attend the Conference at Borgå is certainly a disappointment, but I interpret it thus, that the Lord will bring blessing through another." And in his diary we find the characteristic words: "Can't understand God's ways, but need not." Baron Nicolay followed the progress of the Conference by means of the many letters he received from delegates. His thoughts and prayers embraced every single speech and every critical moment, and they reached their goal, for the universal impression of the Conference was that Baron Nicolay's presence had never seemed so real as now when he was not there. At the close of the Conference he was visited by one of his young friends, Pastor A. Lehtonen, who gave him a verbal report of the days at Borgå, as well as of the Northern Student Conference which had been held in Denmark in August.

The doctors had now declared the disease itself to be over, but a great weakness still overpowered him. On

September 25th, the "critical day" of the year, Baron Nicolay sat up waiting for the great event he longed for. "No, not yet," he wrote that evening in his diary. It seemed for a few days as if his strength was beginning to return. Even when forced to stay in bed he had not been willing to be idle, but read proof for an edition of his pamphlet on the Divinity of Christ which was to be published in Sweden. Now he devoted himself with renewed energy to all the work which he could do while convalescing, spending an entire day packing Russian books to be sent to America to be printed in new editions. On the 30th he came down to dinner for the first time, but going up and down the steep steps which led to his room proved too much of an exertion. For the second time since he was taken ill he was seized in the night of October 2nd by a severe attack of asthma, an entry about this event being the last written with his own hand in his diary. On the same day as the books were sent off he wrote to several people—to Prince Bernadotte about the Conference at Borgå, to Miss Marie Bréchet, Countess Pahlen, his sister, and Father Joseph de Broglie, a French cousin, remembering them especially as they were ill—and a day later followed greetings to Baron K. A. Wrede:

"Thanks, dear friend, for your most welcome lines. May you return with joy and blessing to your work at Helsingfors. To me this is a time of testing and of discipline from the Lord. I have been ill for six weeks, and now, as I was beginning to get better, was attacked with asthma, more violently than ever before, and by a rising temperature. God alone knows if I will ever be

able to continue my former work. Give my warmest
regards to Gertrude. I am now ill in bed again.

"Affectionately your old friend,

"PAUL."

No definite indication of the writer's consciousness
of his approaching departure is found here. Neither
did he drop any remark to that effect to his sisters, who
cared for him tenderly, and sought to ease his pain and
help him pass the time. Only to Pastor Valkama did
he once say: "I know not how this illness will end, but
when God calls me I am ready." He was very grateful
to all around him, and developed a wonderful patience
in his affliction.

On the night before October 6th came the third and
last attack of asthma. Neither ice nor medicine availed.
And shortly before one o'clock in the morning the fight
was over, and, in the presence of his sisters, Paul Nicolay, without a sigh, went quietly to sleep.

The Master he was waiting for had at last come—
not to the world, but to one of the souls who belonged
to Him.

All who knew and loved him were deeply grieved to
learn of Baron Nicolay's death. But while some only
felt the emptiness without him, and could not understand the purpose of God's calling one of His best
workers home at such a difficult time, others realised
that the measure of Paul Nicolay's suffering and toil
on earth had been filled, and that he was ripe for the
rest in the arms of the Father. And many—those
who had been closest to him—felt that *rest* was not to be

the only accompaniment of death, but that God could still use His servant in other and greater ways. Paul Nicolay himself had once said of a friend who was called away just as he was about to undertake a new and blessed work: "Why should God do it? But *promoted* must be the right term to employ about her." The same thought is found in a letter written after his death by the friend who understood him better than any other. To the sisters of Baron Nicolay Mr. Wilder wrote:[1]

"We have learned from Dr. Karl Fries in Sweden of your good brother being called away to a higher service. The news was a great blow to me, as I had hoped to see Paul in our little home in Norway next summer. . . .

"It is well with Paul, for as the great Apostle states, 'To depart and be with Christ is far better.' Have you noticed how the great Apostle after whom Paul was named described death? 'The time of my departure is at hand,'[2] he says. The word translated *departure* in the Greek is *analusis,* a nautical term. Death to Paul was a sailing out onto a sea of great opportunity and privilege, not a coming into port for rest. Tennyson has evidently borrowed his thought from St. Paul in the words:

> " 'Sunset and evening star
> And one clear call for me.
> And may there be no moaning at the bar
> When I put out to sea.' "

---

[1] Quoted from the English letter.
[2] II Timothy 4:6.

To Baron Nicolay's family who remembered him as the eager young sailor, this picture given by his friend became very precious. As time passed, the more did they also experience how true was the thought expressed by another friend in a reminiscence of him: that death does not separate us from him who is "on the other side of Christ," but only veils him from our sight.[1]

October 11, 1919, Baron Nicolay was laid to rest in the grave at Ludwigstein which he had had prepared during his lifetime. A great number of friends had come to Monrepos to be with him on this his last voyage on earth. One who was then present, Mme. Helmi Gulin, has written a description of it in which she succeeded in catching something of the quiet beauty of the event.

"In autumn attire stood the lovely park of Monrepos on October 11th. Heavy and moist, as if tear dewed, hung the yellow leaves on the aged trees. Nature had garbed herself in mourning. A sign of mourning also was the black flag covering the family arms over the door of entrance, and the catafalque wreathed with laurel in the centre of the court-yard. In the large and silent rooms where ancient art and memories of the past greet you at every step, and where all was now in order for the ceremony, it seemed strangely silent. It was not a sense of sorrow and death, but something

[1] Of comfort also were these words found in his diary for 1904: "If God takes me, I want my people to look upon it not as a sad but a joyful event, not to look with carnal eyes at the visible side, but to think that I have dropped my earthly shell and my soul is free and in the glorious presence of Jesus Christ. . . . If I could by prayer prolong my life on earth, I would not."

like a breath of eternity which was felt on approaching one of the music rooms. There he lay, the noble man of the humble heart and with his child-like faith in God, fallen asleep in death. In his flower-bedecked casket, surrounded by the portraits of his forefathers, reposed the last male descendant of his line. . . .

"Long before the hour appointed for the interment a continuous stream of friends, acquaintances, and dependents wandered towards the peaceful resting place. Both old and young, and children from the possessions of Monrepos, all came with their simple tribute of flowers to take a last farewell of their beloved master. And on every face seemed to linger a gleam of the peace of the departed one. How real became the words read by the German Pastor Wegener at the open coffin: 'If our earthly house of this tabernacle were dissolved, we have a building of God, an house not made with hands, *eternal* in the heavens.' For a while the sisters' look lingered on those beloved features, before they were to be hidden away until the Resurrection morning.

"While the children of Monrepos shyly, with their tiny clear voices, sang a hymn, their benefactor was borne for the last time through the rooms of his childhood's home. In the courtyard he was greeted by the song of the school children of Sorvali. And after the coffin was lowered onto the catafalque, around which the volunteer fire corps of Monrepos stood guard with banners of mourning, followed a homage of flowers in token of what the life of the departed had been in sacrificing himself for the good of others. One deputation after another came forward, and in every speech was felt an undertone of deep loss and gratitude.

"When the impressive ceremony in the court-yard was over, twilight had already set in. Through the park the coffin was now borne towards the burial island of Ludwigstein, whose grey monuments were dimly visible against the dark sky. In front of the coffin walked the Bishop of the Diocese, and slowly was the approach made to the shore where the ferry waited. While the choir of the Swedish Church sang: 'Jerusalem, bort fran Jordens grus' (Jerusalem, away from the sorrow of earth), the ferry glided slowly away from the shore. For the last time the owner of Monrepos was now being brought to his beloved Ludwigstein, where he so often used to go at sunset to listen to the splash of the waves or the gentle song of the Æolian harps in the tower. Now they were singing to his own spirit in its flight.

"Like an echo from another world sounded from the mountain top the song of the deaconesses as the coffin was carried up from the ferry: 'Tidehvarf komma, Tidehvarf forsvinna, släckte folger släcktes gång,' and, as twilight deepened the coffin was borne along the mountain path to the foot of the tower. There the service was conducted by Bishop Colliander who spoke on Philippians 3:7-14, words which so well applied to the life of him who had gone home. The darkness increased, and sadly rustled the tall fir trees as the coffin was once more lifted and carried down the steep slope to the spot nearer the shore, which Baron Nicolay had selected for his last resting place. As in a dream we followed. Now they turned to the right, and in deep silence the son was borne past the open vault of his parents' tomb. A few more steps, and the coffin was lowered. And behold! Just then the moon rose above the horizon, sending silvery paths across the water toward the grave. Was it not as if heaven had opened, shedding a gleam of that light which now surrounds the departed one into the hearts of the mourners? And in the quiet of the evening could be heard Pastor Wegener's voice: 'Eye hath not seen, nor ear heard, neither hath entered into the heart of man, the things which God hath prepared for them that love Him.' Beloved eyes are closed forever, eyes which could wear so serious and yet so loving a look, but they have closed only to open in a new, a better, a more glorious world. And that mouth, which through its testimony had led so many to the Lord, is silenced, but only to sing praises in that land where death is swallowed up in victory.

" 'Überwunden der Erde Leid,
Überwunden der Seele Streit,
Rein erfunden vor Gottes Thron,
Teuer erkauft durch Gottes Sohn,
Reingewaschen durch Jesu Blut,
Wohl dir, wohl dir, du hast es gut.

" 'In weissen Kleide im Tempel des Herrn,
Mit Friedenspalmen, dem Morgenstern,
Mit Lebenskronen aus Jesu Hand,
'Mein Kind' aus dem Munde des Höchsten genannt—
Durch Kämpfen zum Sieg,
Durch Glauben zum Schauen,
Überwunden der Kampf und das Todesgrauen,
Überwunden im Glauben durch Jesu Blut,
Wohl dir, wohl dir, du hast es gut.'

" 'Peace, perfect peace,' resounded the last song of the choir by the side of the grave. In peace, perfect peace, rests now the weary warrior with battles passed. What he once said of the hardships and sufferings of life—'Our light affliction, which is but for a moment, worketh for us a far more exceeding and eternal weight of glory'—was so soon to become a reality for him. The peace of the autumn night envelops Monrepos. Still sounds from the tower the gentle song of the Æolian harp, like notes of peace from the eternal world. Peace envelops the flower-bedecked grave. The noble man, who in himself was *nothing* but to whom Christ was *everything,* has gone into a greater light, into the presence of the Master he so faithfully loved and served, and of whose glory his life will continue to witness long after his death."

Soli Deo Gloria

Nothing in himself; this phrase which often means so little to us has a real significance when applied to Paul Nicolay. To his own nature may be ascribed the shortcomings that were his through life, while all the good which radiated from him, and all the good he accomplished, was given him from above. Not that nature had given him a worse equipment than others; as we have seen he started life with all the qualifications which go to make an able, useful person—he had a sound judgment, a pure and noble character, and a social position which was calculated to develop his talents. But this man, who was not a genius, succeeded in the Czar's Russia in establishing a Movement and creating an organisation which would seem to require an unusually gifted founder. This reserved and timid recluse succeeded in gathering scores of people around one great ideal and scattering sunshine across their paths, which is seldom granted to any but the most devout children of life; and, although no orator, his words penetrated deeper and farther than most. These facts of his life are inconceivable and unaccountable, unless one looks beyond the tool to the Master and gives the glory to God alone.

"A tool in the hand of the Lord," was what Paul Nicolay himself longed to be, and had he known that the story of his life should be written, his heartfelt desire concerning it might well have been expressed in

248

the words of the poet: "One does not seek for arrows that have been shot, and the hammer which has been thrown aside." Therefore not without hesitation, was it decided to break the silence enveloping him, neither was it with a light heart that the authoress of this work took up her task. The silence was broken, and the life of Paul Nicolay written for the same reason as the words immortalising his own soul's story in the pages of his diary—*this book is primarily the account of God's work through a weak and frail man who had unreservedly given his life into His hands.*

ON THE ISLE OF DEATH [1]

The waves do whisper it,
The fir trees murmur it,
The flowers waft it,
Whither and how?

The rocks in their brooding
Incline themselves, gazing
Down on those wandering—
Whither and how?

Many have wandered here
Living and laughing—
Many have been borne here,
Silent in death.

The graves they do ask it,
Gently, how quietly—
The heart in its wondering
Finds no reply.

Pause, then, thou wanderer!
Seest 'twixt the rocks there
The grave, which now seemeth
A slumberer's rest?

Marked by the symbol
Of sorrow and victory—
The cross—from his labours
Reposes he here.

[1] This poem written at Baron Nicolay's grave is added to the biography by request. Translated by R.E.W.

250

Here? Thou recallest
The question eternal:
Where is the absent one?
Whither and how?

Turn from the grave now
Thine eyes to the distance,
To the sea which reflecteth
The light of the skies.

Evening approaches—
The sun as it sinketh
Now tinteth golden
The fast fleeting cloud.

Whispering of waves, and
Murmuring of fir trees,
Wondering heart—
Is all silenced now?

Hushed in interminable
Light, thou readest
The answer for him
Who is marked by the Cross.

The answer, the deep
And powerful answer:
Found in Christ Jesus,
From God and to God.

Ludwigstein, June 21, 1921.

THE END